The Literary Cat

The Literary Cat

Walter Chandoha

J. B. LIPPINCOTT COMPANY
Philadelphia and New York

Grateful acknowledgment is made for the use of copyrighted material as follows:

Bill Adams, "Curiosity": Reprinted from *Cats* Magazine by permission of the author.

Lloyd Alexander, "Cat Postures": From *My Five Tigers* by Lloyd Alexander. Copyright © 1956 by Lloyd Alexander. Reprinted by permission of the publishers, E. P. Dutton, and Brandt & Brandt.

Richard Armour, "Cats May Have Nine Lives but I Have Only One": Reprinted by permission of the author.

Margaret Benson, "The Cat Is a Dramatist": Reprinted from *The Soul of a Cat* by permission of G. P. Putnam's Sons.

Lilian Jackson Braun, "Cats' Gifts": Reprinted by permission of the author and her agent, Blanche C. Gregory, Inc. Copyright © 1966 by Lilian Jackson Braun.

Louis Bromfield, "Farm Cats": Reprinted from *Animals and Other People* by Louis Bromfield. Copyright 1947, 1948 by Louis Bromfield. By permission of Harper & Row, Publishers, Inc.

Heywood Broun, "A Cat Is Nobody's Fool": Reprinted by permission of Harcourt Brace Jovanovich, Inc., from "Marion the Cat" in *It Seems to Me*, 1925–35 by Heywood Broun.

Jean Burden: "How to Get a Cat Out of a Tree," reprinted by permission of Woman's Day Magazine. © 1973 by Fawcett Publications, Inc. "A Leavetaking," reprinted by permission of Woman's Day Magazine. Copyright © 1972 by Fawcett Publications, Inc.

Eva Byron, "Cat, Sleeping": Copyright 1942 by Saturday Review Associates. Reprinted by permission of *Saturday Review*.

Elizabeth Coatsworth, "Sunday": Reprinted by permission; © 1939, 1967 The New Yorker Magazine, Inc.

William Cole, "What Could It Be?": Reprinted from *A Cat-Hater's Handbook* by William Cole by permission of the author.

Nelson Antrim Crawford, "Cats and Man Hunt for Sport": Reprinted from *Cats in Prose and Verse* by Nelson Antrim Crawford by permission of Coward, McCann & Geoghegan, Inc.

Mazo de la Roche, "The Ninth Life": Used by permission of the executor and trustee of the Estate of Mazo de la Roche.

Sidney Denham, "Playing with a Cat" and "Cats as Mothers": Reprinted from *Our Cats* by Sidney Denham by permission of Kaye & Ward Ltd.

Eleanor Farjeon, "Cats": Copyright © 1960 by Eleanor Farjeon. From the book *The Children's Bells*, published by Henry Z. Walck Company, Inc., a division of David McKay Company, Inc. Reprinted by permission of the publishers.

William Faulkner, "Cats": From *The Reivers* by William Faulkner. Copyright © 1962 by William Faulkner. Reprinted by permission of Random House, Inc.

H. W. Fowler, "If I Had a Cat": Reprinted by permission of George Allen & Unwin Ltd. from *If Wishes Were Horses* by H. W. Fowler.

H. G. Frommer, "Canine vs. Feline": Reprinted by permission of the *Milwaukee Journal*.

Paul Gallico: "Jennie's Lessons to Peter on How to Behave Like a Cat," from *The Abandoned* by Paul Gallico. Copyright 1950 by Paul Gallico. Reprinted by permission of Alfred A. Knopf, Inc., and Harold Ober Associates, Inc. "Strays," taken from *Honorable Cat* by Paul Gallico. © 1972 by Paul Gallico and Mathemata Anstalt. Used by permission of Crown Publishers, Inc.

Georgina Stickland Gates, "The Modern Cat," "Falling Cat," and "The Cat's Claws": Reprinted from *The Modern Cat: Her Mind and Manners* by permission of the author.

Baron Ireland, "Krazy: Reflection No. 1": From *Our Cat* by Baron Ireland. Copyright 1933 by Nate Salsbury. Used by permission of Doubleday & Company, Inc., and May S. Salsbury.

Louise Lessin, "Cats Train Their Kittens": Reprinted from *Cats and Their People in Haiku* by Louise Lessin by permission of Paul S. Eriksson, Publisher.

Vachel Lindsay, "The Mysterious Cat": Reprinted from *Collected Poems* by Vachel Lindsay. Copyright 1914 by Macmillan Publishing Company, Inc., renewed 1942 by Elizabeth C. Lindsay.

Frances and Richard Lockridge, "A Cat Will Not Be Bullied" and "The Cat's Behavior in Two Worlds": From *Cats and People* by Frances and Richard Lockridge. Copyright 1950 by Frances and Richard Lockridge. Reprinted by permission of J. B. Lippincott Company.

E. V. Lucas, "The Cat's Seriousness": Reprinted by permission of Chatto and Windus Ltd. and the Estate of E. V. Lucas from *A Cat Book* by E. V. Lucas.

don marquis, "eight of my lives are gone" and "mehitabel meets her mate"; From *the lives and times of archy & mehitabel* by don marquis. Copyright 1927 by Doubleday & Company, Inc. Used by permission of the publishers.

Rod McKuen, "A Cat Named Sloopy": From *Listen to the Warm* by Rod McKuen. Copyright © 1967 by Rod McKuen. Reprinted by permission of Random House, Inc.

Faith McNulty and Elizabeth Keiffer, "Cats' Eyes": From *Wholly Cats* by Faith McNulty and Elizabeth Keiffer. Copyright © 1962. Used by permission of Bobbs-Merrill Co., Inc.

Ida M. Mellen, "Facial Expressions": From *The Science and the Mystery of the Cat* by Ida M. Mellen. Used by permission of Charles Scribner's Sons.

Fernand Méry, "The Hypocrisy of Cats?" and "Qualities of Cats": Reprinted by permission of S. G. Phillips, Inc., from *Her Majesty the Cat* by Fernand Méry © 1957.

Christopher Morley, "In Honor of Taffy Topaz": From *Songs for a Little House* by Christopher Morley. Copyright 1917, renewed 1945 by Christopher Morley. Reprinted by permission of J. B. Lippincott Company.

Ogden Nash, "The Kitten": From *Verses from 1929 On* by Ogden Nash. Copyright 1940 by Ogden Nash. Used by permission of Little, Brown and Co.

Laura Riley, "Teaching Cats Tricks": Used by permission of the author.

Damon Runyon, "Cats Are Like Women": Reprinted by permission of American Play Co. from *Guys & Dolls* by Damon Runyon.

May Swenson, "Drawing the Cat": Reprinted by permission of the author, copyright © 1967 in *Half Sun Half Sleep* by May Swenson.

Gladys Taber, "Cat vs Dog": From *Amber, a Very Personal Cat* by Gladys Taber. Copyright © 1970 by Gladys Taber. Reprinted by permission of J. B. Lippincott Company.

Doreen Tovey, "Solomon the Great": From *Cats in the Belfry* by Doreen Tovey. Copyright © 1957 by Doreen Tovey. Used by permission of Doubleday & Company, Inc.

Carl Van Vechten, "The Exemplary Cat": From *The Tiger in the House* by Carl Van Vechten. Copyright 1920, 1936 by Carl Van Vechten. Reprinted by permission of Alfred A. Knopf, Inc.

Dereck Williamson, "Mad Anthony": Used by permission of the author.

Era Zistel, "The Cat That Could": Copyright 1974 New York News Inc. Reprinted by permission.

U.S. Library of Congress Cataloging in Publication Data

Chandoha, Walter.
  The literary cat.

  1. Cats—Addresses, essays, lectures.   2. Cats—
Literary collections.   3. Cats—Pictorial works.
I. Title.
SF445.5.C45   828'.07   77-4679
ISBN-0-397-01213-6

For ENRICO
Who likes cats as much as they like him

INTRODUCTION

As a professional photographer specializing in fauna and flora, I am often asked what animal is my favorite. The big cats of Africa, probably. But since I've spent so little time with them and so much time with the domestic variety, my perennial favorite is the cat in our homes and on our farms.

Of all domestic animals the cat is the most expressive. His face is capable of showing a wide range of expressions. His tail is a mirror of his mind. His gracefulness is surpassed only by his agility. And, along with all these, he has a sense of humor. These are some of the qualities that make the cat an ideal camera subject.

With my photographs I have attempted to show some of the many facets of the cat. Some years ago when I was completing my second cat book, I felt that at last I had photographed the cat in every conceivable pose, posture and situation and there was nothing more to do.

How wrong I was! Now, some 60,000 cat photographs—and a half-dozen cat books—later, I know I'll never be able to completely document the cat. He's too complex a critter.

But I'll keep trying. In studying and photographing cats for over thirty years, I have acquired two of their more admirable traits— tenacity and persistence!

MAD ANTHONY

The tall weeds of September remind me of Mad Anthony, who people said was a little crazy. They were wrong. Mad Anthony was my cat, and I knew he was a lot crazy.

Mad Anthony liked high grass and watering cans. And he liked playing dog.

On a day like this, I would whistle up Mad Anthony, and he would climb out of his watering can where he sat and thought about being a dog. He would trot up to me and wag his tail. Then we'd go for a walk, just a boy and his little furry dog along a country road.

We would stop to look at butterflies and bugs and birds. Mad Anthony would heel. Sometimes he would point. But once in a while he'd get excited, forget he was playing dog, and revert to his natural role of insane cat. He would spring.

Mad Anthony was the only cat I knew who sprang straight up. He never leaped toward a butterfly, bug, or bird. He rose vertically, at least two feet, often three. Whether there was wildlife nearby or not. There was no warning, and the effect was startling. When Mad Anthony sprang, it was as if he'd been standing on a land mine, or over one of those off–on Yellowstone geysers. All of a sudden—*boingg!!*

People were amazed. They asked me why my cat leaped up that way for no reason. I told them he was a very special cat. Privately, I thought it was because he was nuts. But I didn't say that, because I didn't want to hurt his feelings.

We were good friends. We played a game in the tall grass. Mad Anthony scurried into the field and hid. But not too well. He twitched his tail, so I could see weeds moving. Then I ran into the field, straight at him. *Boingg!*—Mad Anthony rocketed up, legs outstretched, mouth wide open, a wild gleam in his slanty eyes.

9

I caught him in my arms. He always pretended to be surprised. He yelled "Yeow!" a couple of times. Then he struggled to get down, so he could run off and do it over again.

The game could take up most of the day. My mother would ask me where I'd been, and I'd say catching the cat.

Mad Anthony lived in the watering can. We left it out all winter for him. He spent an awful lot of time in there. I wondered what he found to do. My parents said he was probably redecorating.

Early in the morning I would tiptoe out of the house and try to sneak up on Mad Anthony. But he always heard me. His head would pop up under the watering-can handle, and he'd squint into the sunshine. His triangular face reminded me of Sub-Mariner, a comic-book hero then.

My family didn't use Mad Anthony's watering can. We bought another one to water the garden with. But one time, somebody got mixed up and put water in Mad Anthony's house while he was out *boingg*-ing around somewhere. He came dashing across the lawn and leaped into the can. There was a terrible splash. And a long pause.

Then the Sub-Mariner's dripping head appeared in the opening. His eyes were more squinty than usual. But he didn't say anything; he just looked casually around, pretending he wasn't up to his neck in water. He stayed in there for a long while, just to make his point. Like I said, he was crazy.

I wish he were still around. Now, a lot of years later, I still think of Mad Anthony when I see tall grass. Or a watering can. But I never see a cat face peeking out. If I did, I guess I'd spring straight in the air.

Dereck Williamson

HOW TO GET A CAT OUT OF A TREE

Some people say that cats get hungry up a tree and that food will often lure the wanderers back to earth. Others maintain that water played on them from above (sometimes quite impossible) will force them down. It has worked with some cats. But all cats? I'm not so sure. Why does the cat go up, anyway? Curiosity? Birds? Of course. But there are other reasons and they remain inexplicable. Does Puss decide to make the trek because it's there? It has been fairly well determined that many cats find some kind of security in high places, perhaps because they are safely out of reach of creatures like dogs.

Whatever the reasons, cats will go on climbing, as they've been doing these many centuries, and some humans will go on sounding alarms while others of us will insist that the alarms are ridiculous and that the cat will, eventually, come down.

Jean Burden

MYSTERIOUS KIND OF FOLK

Cats are a mysterious kind of folk—
there is more passing in their minds
than we are aware of.

Sir Walter Scott

15

THE ROAMING CAT

STATE OF ILLINOIS
EXECUTIVE DEPARTMENT
SPRINGFIELD, APRIL 23, 1949

To the Honorable, the Members of the Senate of the 66th General Assembly:

I herewith return, without my approval, Senate Bill No. 93 entitled "An Act to Provide Protection to Insectivorous Birds by Restraining Cats." This is the so-called "Cat Bill." I veto and withhold my approval from this Bill for the following reasons:

It would impose fines on owners or keepers who permitted their cats to run at large off their premises. It would permit any person to capture, or call upon the police to pick up and imprison, cats at large. . . . This legislation has been introduced in the past several sessions of the Legislature, and it has, over the years, been the source of much comment—not all of which has been in a serious vein. . . . I cannot believe there is a widespread public demand for this law or that it could, as a practical matter, be enforced.

Furthermore, I cannot agree that it should be the declared public policy of Illinois that a cat visiting a neighbor's yard or crossing the highway is a public nuisance. It is in the nature of cats to do a certain amount of unescorted roaming. . . . Also consider the owner's dilemma: To escort a cat abroad on a leash is against the nature of the cat, and to permit it to venture forth for exercise unattended into a night of new dangers is against the nature of the owner. Moreover, cats perform useful service, particularly in rural areas, in combating rodents—work they necessarily perform alone and without regard for property lines. . . .

The problem of cat *versus* bird is as old as time. If we attempt to resolve it by legislation who knows but what we may be called upon to take sides as well in the age-old problem of dog *versus* cat, bird *versus* bird, or even bird *versus* worm. In my opinion, the State of Illinois and its local governing bodies already have enough to do without trying to control feline delinquency.

For these reasons, and not because I love birds the less or cats the more, I veto and withhold my approval from Senate Bill No. 93.

Respectfully,

Adlai E. Stevenson, Governor

THE NINTH LIFE

She could see the twinkling lights of the town across the bay, when her pain came on. It was so piercing, so sudden, that she turned, with a savage cry, to face what seemed to be attacking her in the rear. But then she knew that the pain was inside her.

She lay writhing on the ground and before long gave birth to a kitten. She began to lick it, then realized that it was dead. She ran on toward the town as fast as she could.

She was still two miles from it when she had two more kittens. She lay beside them for a while, feeling weak and peaceful. Now the lights of the town were out. Harriet picked up one of the kittens and limped on. With it in her mouth she went along the paved street. She gave a meow of delight as she reached the back door of her own home.

She laid the kitten on the doorstep and herself began limping back and forth, the length of the step, rubbing her sides against the door. For the first time since she had been left on the island she purred. The purr bubbled in her throat, vibrating through her nerves in an ecstasy of home-coming. She caressed the back door with every bit of her. She stood on her hind legs and caressed the door handle with a loving paw. Only the weak cry of her kitten made her desist.

She carried it to the tool shed and laid it on the mat where the terrier slept in warm weather. She laid herself down beside it, trilling to it in love. It buried its sightless face against her lank belly. She lay flat on her side, weary to the bone.

Mazo de la Roche

18

JENNIE'S LESSONS TO PETER
ON HOW TO BEHAVE LIKE A CAT

"Jennie, why when you are pleased and happy and relaxed, do your claws work in and out in that queer way? Once back home—I mean when we lived in the warehouse—I noticed that you were moving your paws up and down, almost as though you were making the bed. I never do that, though I do purr when I am happy."

Jennie was lying on her side on the canvas hatch cover when Peter asked that question, and she raised her head and gave him a most tender glance before she replied: "I know, Peter. And it is just another of those things that tell me that in spite of your shape and form, you are really human, and perhaps always will be. But maybe I can explain it to you. Peter, say something sweet to me."

The only thing Peter could think of to say was: "Oh, Jennie, I wish that I could be all cat—so that I might be more like you."

The most beatific smile stole over Jennie's face. Her throat throbbed with purring, and slowly her white paws began to work, the claws moving in and out as though she were kneading dough.

"You see?" she said to Peter. "It has to do with feeling happy. It goes all the way back to our being kittens and being nursed by our mothers. We cannot even see at first, but only feel, for when we are first born we are blind, and our eyes open only after a few weeks. But we can feel our way to our mother's breast and bury ourselves in her soft, sweet-smelling fur to find her milk, and when we are there, we work our paws gently up and down to help the food we want so much to flow more freely. Then when it does, we feel it in our throats, warm and satisfying; it stops our hunger and our thirst, it soothes our fears and desires, and oh, Peter, we are *so* blissful and contented at that moment, so secure and peaceful and—well, just happy. We never forget those moments with our mothers. They remain with us all the rest of our lives. And later on, long after we are grown, when something makes us very happy, our paws and claws go in and out the same way, in memory of those early times of our first real happiness. And that is all I can tell you about it."

Paul Gallico,
The Abandoned

THE CAT THAT WALKED BY HIMSELF

This befell and behappened and became and was, O, my Best Beloved, when the tame animals were wild. The Dog was wild, and the Horse was wild, and the Cow was wild, and the Sheep was wild, and the Pig was wild—as wild as could be—and they walked in the wet wild woods by their wild lones, but the wildest of all the wild animals was the Cat. He walked by himself, and all places were alike to him.

Of course the Man was wild too. He was dreadfully wild. He didn't even begin to be tame till he met the Woman and she did not like living in his wild ways. She picked out a nice dry cave, instead of a heap of wet leaves, to lie down in, and she strewed clean sand on the floor, and she lit a nice fire of wood at the back of the cave, and she hung a dried Wild Horse skin, tail down, across the opening of the cave, and she said: "Wipe your feet when you come in, and now we'll keep house."

That night, Best Beloved, they ate Wild Sheep roasted on the hot stones and flavored with wild garlic and wild pepper, and Wild Duck stuffed with wild rice, and wild fenugreek and wild coriander, and marrow-bones of Wild Oxen, and wild cherries and wild grenadillas. Then the Man went to sleep in front of the fire ever so happy, but the Woman sat up, combing her hair. She took the bone of the shoulder of mutton, the big flat blade-bone, and she looked at the wonderful marks on it, and she threw more wood on the fire and she made a magic. She made the first Singing Magic in the world.

Out in the wet wild woods all the wild animals gathered together where they could see the light of the fire a long way off, and they wondered what it meant.

Then Wild Horse stamped with his foot and said: "O, my friends and my enemies, why have the Man and the Woman made that great light in that great cave, and what harm will it do us?"

Wild Dog lifted up his nose and smelled the smell of the roast mutton and said: "I will go up and see and look and stay: for I think it is good. Cat, come with me."

"Nenni," said the Cat. "I am the Cat who walks by himself, and all places are alike to me. I will not come."

"Then we will never be friends again," said Wild Dog, and he trotted off to the cave.

But when he had gone a little way the Cat said to himself: "All places are alike to me. Why should I not go too and see and look and come away?" So he slipped after Wild Dog softly, very softly, and hid himself where he could hear everything.

When Wild Dog reached the mouth of the cave he lifted up the dried Horse skin with his nose a little bit and sniffed the beautiful smell of the roast mutton, and the Woman heard him and laughed and said: "Here comes the First wild thing out of the wild woods. What do you want?"

Wild Dog said: "O, my enemy and wife of my enemy, what is this that smells so good in the wild woods?"

Then the Woman picked up a roasted mutton bone and threw it to Wild Dog and said: "Wild thing out of the wild woods, taste and try." Wild Dog gnawed the bone and it was more delicious than anything he had ever tasted, and he said: "O, my enemy and wife of my enemy, give me another."

The Woman said: "Wild thing out of the wild woods, help my

23

Man to hunt through the day and guard this cave at night and I will give you as many roast bones as you need."

"Ah!" said the Cat listening, "this is a very wise Woman, but she is not so wise as I am."

Wild Dog crawled into the cave and laid his head on the Woman's lap and said: "O, my friend and wife of my friend, I will help your Man to hunt through the day, and at night I will guard your cave."

"Ah!" said the Cat listening, "that is a very foolish Dog." And he went back through the wet wild woods waving his tail and walking by his wild lone. But he never told anybody.

When the Man waked up he said: "What is Wild Dog doing here?" And the Woman said: "His name is not Wild Dog any more, but the First Friend because he will be our friend for always and always and always. Take him with you when you go hunting."

Next night the Woman cut great green armfuls of fresh grass from the water-meadows and dried it before the fire so that it smelt like new-mown hay, and she sat at the mouth of the cave and plaited a halter out of Horse-hide, and she looked at the shoulder of mutton bone—at the big broad blade-bone—and she made a magic. She made the second Singing Magic in the world.

Out in the wild woods all the wild animals wondered what had happened to Wild Dog, and at last Wild Horse stamped with his foot and said: "I will go and see why Wild Dog has not returned. Cat, come with me."

"Nenni," said the Cat. "I am the Cat who walks by himself, and all places are alike to me. I will not come." But all the same he followed Wild Horse softly, very softly, and hid himself where he could hear everything.

When the Woman heard Wild Horse tripping and stumbling on his long mane she laughed and said: "Here comes the Second wild thing out of the wild woods. What do you want?"

Wild Horse said: "O, my enemy and wife of my enemy, where is Wild Dog?"

The Woman laughed and picked up the blade-bone and looked at it and said: "Wild thing out of the wild woods, you did not come here for Wild Dog, but for the sake of this good grass."

And Wild Horse, tripping and stumbling on his long mane, said: "That is true, give it me to eat."

The Woman said: "Wild thing out of the wild woods, bend your

wild head and wear what I give you and you shall eat the wonderful grass three times a day."

"Ah," said the Cat listening, "this is a clever Woman, but she is not so clever as I am."

Wild Horse bent his wild head and the Woman slipped the plaited hide halter over it, and Wild Horse breathed on the Woman's feet and said: "O, my mistress and wife of my master, I will be your servant for the sake of the wonderful grass."

"Ah," said the Cat listening, "that is a very foolish Horse." And he went back through the wet wild woods, waving his wild tail and walking by his wild lone.

When the Man and the Dog came back from hunting the Man said: "What is Wild Horse doing here?" And the Woman said: "His name is not Wild Horse any more, but the First Servant because he will carry us from place to place for always and always and always. Take him with you when you go hunting."

———————

Next day, holding her wild head high that her wild horns should not catch in the wild trees, Wild Cow came up to the cave, and the Cat followed and hid himself just the same as before; and everything happened just the same as before; and the Cat said the same things as before, and when Wild Cow had promised to give her milk to the Woman every day in exchange for the wonderful grass, the Cat went back through the wet wild woods walking by his lone just the same as before.

And when the Man and the Horse and the Dog came home from hunting and asked the same questions, same as before, the Woman said: "Her name is not Wild Cow any more, but the Giver of Good Things. She will give us the warm white milk for always and always and always, and I will take care of her while you three go hunting."

Next day the Cat waited to see if any other wild thing would go up to the cave, but no one moved, so the Cat walked there by himself, and he saw the Woman milking the Cow, and he saw the light of the fire in the cave, and he smelt the smell of the warm white milk.

Cat said: "O, my enemy and wife of my enemy, where did Wild Cow go?"

The Woman laughed and said: "Wild thing out of the wild woods, go back to the woods again for I have braided up my hair and I have put away the blade-bone, and we have no more need of either friends or servants in our cave."

26

Cat said: "I am not a friend and I am not a servant. I am the Cat who walks by himself and I want to come into your cave."

The Woman said: "Then why did you not come with First Friend on the first night?"

Cat grew very angry and said: "Has Wild Dog told tales of me?"

Then the Woman laughed and said: "You are the Cat who walks by himself and all places are alike to you. You are neither a friend nor a servant. You have said it yourself. Go away and walk by yourself in all places alike."

Then the Cat pretended to be sorry and said: "Must I never come into the cave? Must I never sit by the warm fire? Must I never drink the warm white milk? You are very wise and very beautiful. You should not be cruel even to a Cat."

Then the Woman said: "I knew I was wise but I did not know I was beautiful. So I will make a bargain with you. If ever I say one word in your praise you may come into the cave."

"And if you say two words in my praise?" said the Cat.

"I never shall," said the Woman, "but if I say two words you may sit by the fire in the cave."

"And if you say three words?" said the Cat.

"I never shall," said the Woman, "but if I do you may drink the warm white milk three times a day for always and always and always."

Then the Cat arched his back and said: "Now let the curtain at the mouth of the cave, and the fire at the back of the cave, and the milk-pots that stand beside the fire remember what my enemy and the wife of my enemy has said." And he went away through the wet wild woods waving his wild tail and walking by his wild lone.

That night when the Man and the Horse and the Dog came home from hunting, the Woman did not tell them of the bargain that she had made because she was afraid that they might not like it.

———————

Cat went far and far away and hid himself in the wet wild woods by his wild lone for a long time till the Woman forgot all about him. Only the Bat—the little upside-down Bat—that hung inside the cave knew where Cat hid, and every evening he would fly to Cat with the news.

One evening the Bat said: "There is a Baby in the cave. He is new and pink and fat and small, and the Woman is very fond of him."

"Ah," said the Cat listening, "but what is the Baby fond of?"

"He is fond of things that are soft and tickle," said the Bat. "He is fond of warm things to hold in his arms when he goes to sleep. He is fond of being played with. He is fond of all those things."

"Ah," said the Cat, "then my time has come."

Next night Cat walked through the wet wild woods and hid very near the cave till morning-time. The Woman was very busy cooking, and the Baby cried and interrupted; so she carried him outside the cave and gave him a handful of pebbles to play with. But still the Baby cried.

Then the Cat put out his paddy-paw and patted the Baby on the cheek, and it cooed; and the Cat rubbed against its fat knees and tickled it under its fat chin with his tail. And the Baby laughed; and the Woman heard him and smiled.

Then the Bat—the little upside-down Bat—that hung in the mouth of the cave said: "O, my hostess and wife of my host and mother of my host, a wild thing from the wild woods is most beautifully playing with your Baby."

"A blessing on that wild thing whoever he may be," said the Woman, straightening her back, "for I was a busy Woman this morning and he has done me a service."

That very minute and second, Best Beloved, the dried Horse-skin curtain that was stretched tail down at the mouth of the cave fell down—*So!*—because it remembered the bargain, and when the Woman went to pick it up—lo and behold!—the Cat was sitting quite comfy inside the cave.

"O, my enemy and wife of my enemy and mother of my enemy," said the Cat, "it is I, for you have spoken a word in my praise, and now I can sit within the cave for always and always and always. But still I am the Cat who walks by himself and all places are alike to me."

The Woman was very angry and shut her lips tight and took up her spinning-wheel and began to spin.

But the Baby cried because the Cat had gone away, and the Woman could not hush him for he struggled and kicked and grew black in the face.

"O, my enemy and wife of my enemy and mother of my enemy," said the Cat, "take a strand of the thread that you are spinning and tie it to your spindle-wheel and drag it on the floor and I will show you a magic that shall make your Baby laugh as loudly as he is now crying."

"I will do so," said the Woman, "because I am at my wits' end, but I will not thank you for it."

She tied the thread to the little pot spindle-wheel and drew it across the floor and the Cat ran after it and patted it with his paws, and rolled head over heels, and tossed it backward over his shoulder, and chased it between his hindlegs, and pretended to lose it, and pounced down upon it again till the Baby laughed as loudly as he had been crying, and scrambled after the Cat and frolicked all over the cave till he grew tired and settled down to sleep with the Cat in his arms.

"Now," said the Cat, "I will sing the Baby a song that shall keep him asleep for an hour." And he began to purr loud and low, low and loud, till the Baby fell fast asleep. The Woman smiled as she looked down upon the two of them and said: "That was wonderfully done. Surely you are very clever, O, Cat."

That very minute and second, Best Beloved, the smoke of the fire at the back of the cave came down in clouds from the roof because it remembered the bargain, and when it had cleared away—lo and behold!—the Cat was sitting, quite comfy, close to the fire.

"O, my enemy and wife of my enemy and mother of my enemy," said the Cat, "it is I, for you have spoken a second word in my praise, and now I can sit by the warm fire at the back of the cave for always

and always and always. But still I am the Cat who walks by himself
and all places are alike to me."

Then the Woman was very, very angry and let down her hair and
put more wood on the fire and brought out the broad blade-bone of the
shoulder of mutton and began to make a magic that should prevent her
from saying a third word in praise of the Cat. It was not a Singing
Magic, Best Beloved, it was a Still Magic; and by and by the cave grew
so still that a little wee-wee Mouse crept out of a corner and ran across
the floor.

"O, my enemy and wife of my enemy and mother of my enemy,"
said the Cat, "is that little Mouse part of your magic?"

"No," said the Woman, and she dropped the blade-bone and
jumped upon a footstool in front of the fire and braided up her hair
very quick for fear that the Mouse should run up it.

"Ah," said the Cat listening, "then the Mouse will do me no harm
if I eat it?"

"No," said the Woman, braiding up her hair; "eat it quick and I
will always be grateful to you."

31

Cat made one jump and caught the little Mouse, and the Woman said: "A hundred thanks to you, O, Cat. Even the First Friend is not quick enough to catch little Mice as you have done. You must be very wise."

That very moment and second, O, Best Beloved, the milk-pot that stood by the fire cracked in two pieces—*So!*—because it remembered the bargain, and when the Woman jumped down from the footstool—lo and behold!—the Cat was lapping up the warm white milk that lay in one of the broken pieces.

"O, my enemy and wife of my enemy and mother of my enemy," said the Cat, "it is I, for you have spoken three words in my praise, and now I can drink the warm white milk three times a day for always and always and always. But *still* I am the Cat who walks by himself and all places are alike to me."

Then the Woman laughed and set him a bowl of the warm white milk and said: "O, Cat, you are as clever as a Man, but remember that the bargain was not made with the Man or the Dog, and I do not know what they will do when they come home."

"What is that to me?" said the Cat. "If I have my place by the fire and my milk three times a day I do not care what the Man or the Dog can do."

That evening when the Man and the Dog came into the cave the Woman told them all the story of the bargain, and the Man said: "Yes, but he has not made a bargain with me or with all proper Men after me." And he took off his two leather boots and he took up his little stone axe (that makes three) and he fetched a piece of wood and a hatchet (that is five altogether), and he set them out in a row, and he said: "Now we will make a bargain. If you do not catch Mice when you are in the cave, for always and always and always, I will throw these five things at you whenever I see you, and so shall all proper Men do after me."

"Ah," said the Woman listening. "This is a very clever Cat, but he is not so clever as my Man."

The Cat counted the five things (and they looked very knobby) and he said: "I will catch Mice when I am in the cave for always and always and always: but still I am the Cat that walks by himself and all places are alike to me."

"Not when I am near," said the Man. "If you had not said that I would have put all these things away (for always and always and always), but now I am going to throw my two boots and my little stone axe (that makes three) at you whenever I meet you, and so shall all proper Men do after me."

Then the Dog said: "Wait a minute. He has not made a bargain with me." And he sat down and growled dreadfully and showed all his teeth and said: "If you are not kind to the Baby while I am in the cave for always and always and always I will chase you till I catch you, and when I catch you I will bite you, and so shall all proper Dogs do after me."

"Ah," said the Woman listening. "This is a very clever Cat, but he is not so clever as the Dog."

Cat counted the Dog's teeth (and they looked very pointed) and he said: "I will be kind to the Baby while I am in the cave as long as he does not pull my tail too hard for always and always and always. But still I am the Cat that walks by himself and all places are alike to me."

"Not when I am near," said the Dog. "If you had not said that I would have shut my mouth for always and always and always, but now I am going to chase you up a tree whenever I meet you, and so shall all proper Dogs do after me."

Then the Man threw his two boots and his little stone axe (that makes three) at the Cat, and the Cat ran out of the cave and the Dog

chased him up a tree, and from that day to this, Best Beloved, three proper Men out of five will always throw things at a Cat whenever they meet him, and all proper Dogs will chase him up a tree. But the Cat keeps his side of the bargain too. He will kill Mice and he will be kind to Babies when he is in the house, as long as they do not pull his tail too hard. But when he has done that, and between times, he is the Cat that walks by himself and all places are alike to him, and if you look out at nights you can see him waving his wild tail and walking by his wild lone—just the same as before.

Rudyard Kipling,
Just So Stories

eight of my lives are gone

eight of my lives are gone
it s years since my fur was slicked
but blow north wind blow
i m damned if i am licked

don marquis,
the lives and times
of archy and mehitabel

THE TEMPTED CAT

'Twas on a lofty vase's side,
Where China's gayest art had dyed
   The azure flowers that blow;
Demurest of the tabby kind,
The pensive Selima, reclined,
   Gazed on the lake below.

Her conscious tail her joy declared;
The fair round face, the snowy beard,
   The velvet of her paws,
Her coat, that with the tortoise vies,
Her ears of jet, and emerald eyes,
   She saw; and purred applause.

Still had she gazed, but 'midst the tide
Two angel forms were seen to glide,
   The Genii of the stream:
Their scaly armor's Tyrian hue
Through richest purple to the view
   Betrayed a golden gleam.

The hapless Nymph with wonder saw:
A whisker first and then a claw,
   With many an ardent wish,
She stretched, in vain, to reach the prize.
What female heart can gold despise?
   What Cat's averse to fish?

Presumptuous Maid! with looks intent
Again she stretched, again she bent,
   Nor knew the gulf between.
(Malignant Fate sat by and smiled.)

The slippery verge her feet beguiled,
She tumbled headlong in.

Eight times emerging from the flood
She mewed to every watery god,
   Some speedy aid to send.
No Dolphin came, no Nereid stirred:
Nor cruel Tom nor Susan heard,—
   A Favorite has no friend!

From hence, ye Beauties, undeceived,
Know, one false step is ne'er retrieved,
   And be with caution bold.
Not all that tempts your wandering eyes
And heedless hearts, is lawful prize;
   Nor all that glisters, gold.

Thomas Gray

THE CHESHIRE CAT

The Cheshire Cat only grinned when it saw Alice. It looked good-natured, she thought: still it had *very* long claws and a great many teeth, so she felt it ought to be treated with respect.

"Cheshire Puss," she began, rather timidly, as she did not at all know whether it would like the name: however, it only grinned a little wider. "Come, it's pleased so far," thought Alice, and she went on, "Would you tell me, please, which way I ought to walk from here?"

"That depends a good deal on where you want to get to," said the Cat.

"I don't much care where—" said Alice.

"Then it doesn't matter which way you walk," said the Cat.

"—so long as I get *somewhere*," Alice added as an explanation.

"Oh, you're sure to do that," said the Cat, "if you only walk long enough."

Alice felt that this could not be denied, so she tried another question. "What sort of people live about here?"

"In *that* direction," the Cat said, waving its right paw round, "lives a Hatter: and in *that* direction," waving the other paw, "lives a March Hare. Visit either you like: they're both mad."

"But I don't want to go among mad people," Alice remarked.

"Oh, you can't help that," said the Cat: "we're all mad here. I'm mad. You're mad."

"How do you know I'm mad?" said Alice.

"You must be," said the Cat, "or you wouldn't have come here."

Alice didn't think that proved it at all; however, she went on: "and how do you know that you're mad?"

"To begin with," said the Cat, "a dog's not mad. You grant that?"

"I suppose so," said Alice.

"Well then," the Cat went on, "you see a dog growls when it's angry, and wags its tail when it's pleased. Now *I* growl when I'm pleased, and wag my tail when I'm angry. Therefore I'm mad."

Lewis Carroll,
Alice in Wonderland

SUNDAY

This is the day when all through the town
the cats are keeping store,
the clerks are gone from counter and desk,
the key has turned in the door.

But the cats move about with an owner's airs
over the oranges, apples, and pears,
or among the tins in their rows on the shelves,
proud as merchants and nimble as elves.

Then at last they each lie down to rest
where the big show window is sunniest,
or turn to stare at the passer-by
with a calculating but sleepy eye.

In every one of the forty-eight states,
in a thousand cities or more,
from Saturday night to Monday at seven
the cats are keeping store!

Elizabeth Coatsworth

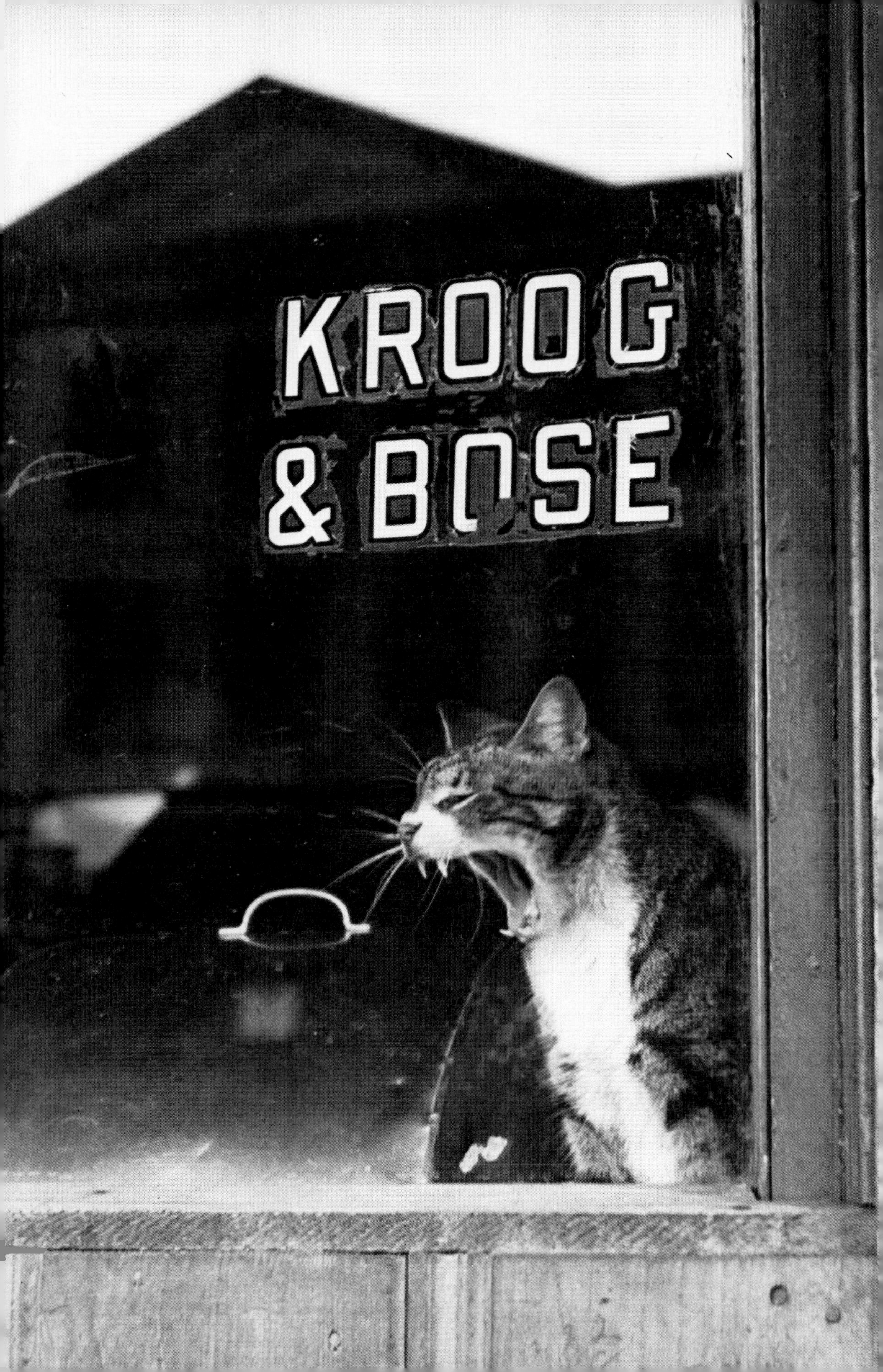
KROOG
& BOSE

THE EXEMPLARY CAT

There is no single quality of the cat that man could not emulate to his advantage. He is clean, the cleanest, indeed, of all animals, absolutely without odor or soil when it is within his power to be so. He is silent, walking on padded paws with claws withdrawn, making no sound unless he wishes to say something definite and then he can express himself freely. . . .

He is entirely self-reliant. . . . If he is suddenly thrown on his own resources in the country he can support himself on the highway; he can even support himself in town under conditions that would terrify . . . the dog. . . .

He is beautiful and he is graceful. He makes his appearance and his life as exquisite as circumstances will permit. He is modest, he is urbane, he is dignified. Indeed, a well-bred cat never argues. He goes about doing what he likes in a well-bred superior manner. If he is interrupted he will look at you in mild surprise or silent reproach but he will return to his desire. If he is prevented, he will wait for a more favorable occasion. But like all well-bred individualists . . . the cat seldom interferes with other people's rights. His intelligence keeps him from doing many of the fool things that complicate life. Cats never write operas and they never attend them. They never sign papers, or pay taxes, or vote for president. An injunction will have no power whatever over a cat. A cat, of course, would not only refuse to obey any amendment whatever to any constitution, he would refuse to obey the constitution itself.

Carl Van Vechten,
The Tiger in the House

CERTAIN CAT CHARACTERISTICS

In many respects cats are more like men and women than dogs; they have moods, and their nature is complex. A dog is a good dog or a bad dog, brave or cowardly. But every cat has a character peculiar to itself. There is more individuality in cats. Cats do not take punishment as dogs do; their tempers rise, and if struck they are apt to strike back; but beyond a gentle cuff to a kitten, now and then, I find a scolding or an exclamation of rebuke enough. They are also less forgiving than a dog if unintentionally stepped on or hurt, and frequently bear a grudge for days toward the person guilty of offence. Cats are exceedingly irritable by temperament, sensitive to changes of the weather, frost, or thunder, and usually afraid of the latter; they are excitable, and naturally disposed to bite and scratch when at play; there is a tendency in them, as in ill-balanced human beings, to lose their heads when in high spirits, and the self-command most of them show when full-grown in resisting these impulses, is a striking proof of conscious responsibility. A full-grown pet cat scarcely ever scratches a young child, no matter how much he is mauled by it, and, indeed, one often notices the same thing in kittens. Besides being irritable, cats are subject to depression, probably a physical reaction from their former condition. Their instinct when ill or sad is to be alone, but this may be neutralized by petting; they become as dependent on caresses and sympathy as children, and much wiser than children when ill or injured, for they ask relief with the most unmistakable suggestions, sometimes indicating plainly where they are in pain, and presenting the suffering member for treatment. They are not so patient as dogs in taking medicine or submitting to surgical care, but they show recognition of its benefit by coming back for it under similar circumstances.

Helen M. Winslow,
Concerning Cats

A CAT WILL NOT BE BULLIED

A cat will not be bullied by anything, on two legs or four, or on multiple legs or no legs at all. The cat will come or not come as suits the cat, the cat will withdraw if it grows bored; no cat will ever suffer politely at a cocktail party. Because of this attitude, the cat is "independent"; he may be termed "anti-social" or even, by some, "stupid." Perhaps it would be more accurate to say that, instead of being primarily any of these things, the cat is selective and that the bases of his selection are not always clear to the human mind.

Frances and Richard Lockridge,
Cats and People

CAT, SLEEPING

Be quiet, mind; lie still; be a cat sleeping in the sun,
A cat asleep in the grass.
Let all things pass
Unheeded; let the field mice run
Through the grain; let the grasshoppers play on the stalks of the plants
     close by;
Lazily open one eye
On marauding birds in the garden, but do not stir—
Lie still and purr.

All night long the cat has hunted the field mice,
Creeping through shadows on wary and soundless paws;
But the field mice evaded her—even with all her cunning
They were too quick for her claws.

And the birds were not caught:
In the cold half-light of the dawning
They saw where she waited, crouching, ready to spring;
Leaving her lashing her tail in a futile fury
The birds took wing—

And she was perforce content with the small grasshoppers,
Too plentiful in the garden, and easy prey—
But even of these, could she conquer a hundred thousand
In a single day?

Oblivious, now, in the grass, in the sunlight, sleeping,
The cat lies curled;
Storing up energy, gathering force for new forays
On the plagues of her world.

Have done for a time, then, mind, with your pouncing and leaping—
Be a cat in the grass, be a cat in the sun, sleeping.

Eva Byron

49

CALVIN: A STUDY OF CHARACTER

As I look back upon it, Calvin's life seems to me a fortunate one, for it was natural and unforced. He ate when he was hungry, slept when he was sleepy, and enjoyed existence to the very tips of his toes and the end of his expressive and slow-moving tail. He delighted to roam about the garden and stroll among the trees, and to lie on the green grass and luxuriate in all the sweet influences of summer. You could never accuse him of idleness, and yet he knew the secret of repose. The poet who wrote so prettily of him that his little life was rounded with a sleep understated his felicity; it was rounded with a good many. His conscience never seemed to interfere with his slumbers. In fact, he had good habits and a contented mind. I can see him now walk in at the study door, sit down by my chair, bring his tail artistically about his feet, and look up at me with unspeakable happiness in his handsome face. I often thought that he felt the dumb limitation which denied him the power of language. But since he was denied speech, he scorned the inarticulate mouthings of the lower animals. The vulgar mewing and yowling of the cat species was beneath him; he sometimes uttered a sort of articulate and well-bred ejaculation, when he wished to call attention to something that he considered remarkable, or to some want of his, but he never went whining about. He would sit for hours at a closed window, when he desired to enter, without a murmur, and when it was opened he never admitted that he had been impatient by "bolting" in. Though speech he had not, and the unpleasant kind of utterance given to his race he would not use, he had a mighty power of purr to express his measureless content with congenial society. There was in him a musical organ with stops of varied power and expression, upon which I have no doubt he could have performed Scarlatti's celebrated cat's-fugue.

Charles Dudley Warner,
My Summer in a Garden

THE CAT'S BEHAVIOR IN TWO WORLDS

As he moves between the two worlds, the cat speaks languages suitable to the comprehension of the other denizens—speaks in one fashion to men and women and in quite another to his fellow cats, and to the mice and birds and, lamentably, dogs who share or intrude upon the feline world. To show affection for another cat, a cat licks it and the greatest affection is shown by licking the other cat's face. When a cat wishes to join another, or several others, in a preempted place—a box, a warm ledge, a cushion—the newcomer must first lick, if only in token, the cats or cats who got there first. Failure to do this is bad manners and may lead to ejection by the resident. Now and then, the cat who has been moved in on may comment audibly, giving permission or expressing disapproval, but this is unusual, even among quite talkative cats. Except in anger or other passion, and as between mother cats and kittens, audible conversation is the exception between cat and cat. Beyond hissing, which is done by curling the tongue up at the sides, making it into a kind of trough, cats have little to say to dogs, and a minor growl will do for a rat or mouse.

But with humans who, as the cat has noticed, communicate with one another by making sounds, almost all cats talk audibly and some talk a good deal. (Siamese are traditionally, and in our experience actually, the most frequent talkers.) They speak abruptly when they want out or want dinner; some of them talk uninterruptedly while their meals are being prepared; they purr when stroked (as, although more rarely, they purr when licked by one another); many of them respond, usually in a monosyllable or two, when spoken to in greeting; Martini has a special quick ejaculation used only when she wishes to jump to human shoulders—it is at once request and warning, although more the latter than the former. If offended by a human, a cat will growl briefly in admonition—as it will with another cat; if sufficiently alarmed by human, as by dog or other cat, a cat will hiss.

Frances and Richard Lockridge,
Cats and People

53

THE CAT IS A DRAMATIST

The cat is, above all things, a dramatist; its life is living in an endless romance though the drama is played out on quite another stage than our own, and we only enter into it as subordinate characters, as stage managers, or rather stage carpenters.

We realize this with kittens; we see that the greater part of their life, of the sights and sounds of it, are the material of a drama half-consciously played; they are determined to make mysteries, and as a child will seize upon the passing light or shadow to help him to transform some well-known object into the semblance of living creature, so you may see the kitten reach a paw again and again to touch a reflection on a polished floor, or conjure the shadows of evening into the forms of enemies.

We cannot but see this, and our mistake comes later when the kitten passes partly out of our ken to reappear from time to time, a serious, furtive creature with the weight of the world on its shoulders. We think then that the romance has ceased, when it has in reality gone deeper; the stage has widened out of sight, and if the cat no longer plays before us it is because we have lost sympathy with this side of its life; if we encourage it, it will play like a kitten up to old age. This same fact possibly explains the reason of the theory that cats care for places and not for people—it may be because these same people care for kittens and not for cats; thus the cat transfers the affection it might have felt for the human being to the scene of its romances and the places where it has experienced the surprise and joy of its kittens.

Margaret Benson,
The Soul of a Cat

CATS AND MAN HUNT FOR SPORT

Many persons are surprised also to learn that well-fed cats are the best mousers. Doubtless there was a time when the ancestors of the present domesticated cats hunted in order to obtain enough food to keep alive. Certainly this is true of the leopard, the tiger, the panther, and other wild members of the feline family, although it is noticeable that even these get tremendous pleasure through playing with the game that they catch. The domestic cat, long-haired or short-haired, has been domesticated for so many centuries—longer, presumably, than any other animal—and has received so much attention from cat-lovers that the sporting instinct, rather than hunger, causes it to catch mice, rats, and other small animals. Innumerable cats do not even deign to eat their game. In the process of social evolution they have undergone a change comparable to that of civilized man, who hunts for pleasure rather than a livelihood.

Nelson Antrim Crawford,
Cats in Prose and Verse

SOLOMON THE GREAT

Solomon, however, even as a kitten, had a voice only to be compared with a bullfrog. And he never stopped talking. We used to hear him sometimes talking in the middle of the night. When we went in to see what was wrong—we never ignored noises in the night since the time we found Blondin hanging behind a door, trying to suffocate himself in the sleeve-lining of a coat—there, invariably, were the other three kittens snoring away peacefully like little white angels, Sugieh lying on her side with one eye open, obviously wishing him to the devil—and Solomon, bolt upright in the basket, talking to a spider on the wall.

Solomon loved spiders. When he found one too old or infirm to get away he ate it noisily with his mouth open—a habit he had inherited from Sugieh—talking and chewing appreciatively at the same time. It took us quite a time to discover which kitten it was who gave an ecstatic "Woohoohoo" at intervals while eating rabbit, like a small damp train going through the Rockies, but in the end that turned out to be Solomon too.

He had a vocabulary all his own, which for our own good we quickly learned to understand. A black head appearing round the living room door when we had company and uttering a small but urgent "Wooooh" meant he was sorry to intrude but the earth-box was dirty, and he wanted it changed in a hurry. Solomon didn't like dirty earth-boxes. A raucous "Waaow" accompanied by banging noises from the kitchen as he tried valiantly to open the pantry door meant that he was hungry. Loud and prolonged wailing from somewhere up on the hillside behind the cottage meant that Solomon, after setting out with the others all bluff and bustle and Head of the Family, had once more got left behind and wanted to be rescued. The only time he couldn't talk was when he was feeding from Sugieh and if he opened his mouth he lost his place. Then, instead of talking, he waggled his big bat ears so frantically he looked as if he were about to take off.

Doreen Tovey,
Cats in the Belfry

STRAYS

Is there a more pitiable creature in the realm of four-footed animals than the stray cat, foodless, shelterless, harried through the back alleys and slums of the cities of the world?

The lost or abandoned dog of the streets, searching with haunted eyes into human faces for someone who will be friend and master again, wrings the heart too. But how dare one think of beasts as long as there is still a single child in the world, its body clad in rags, its stomach distended by starvation, its limbs maimed, orphaned or abandoned, staring its silent reproach at one from page or flickering screen?

And yet somehow it is the homeless cat that has become the byword for misery and wretchedness and which daily holds up the mirror to human conscienceless neglect of all that suffer.

And so this derelict impinges upon my awareness, because it is there. I see it daily, gaunt, bedraggled, dirty, its ribs showing through matted fur, sores on its body and eyes, hungry, frightened, defeated, and it breaks my heart.

It is cold when I am warm, starving when I am sated, wet and shivering in the rain and hail when I am dry and safe, abandoned when I am afforded love and companionship. Nothing softens or ameliorates its life of hardship and squalor: its birthplace and burial ground a refuse heap.

It is, I think, the fall from high estate that makes its plight so vivid and painful. For by nature it is fastidious, gregarious, clean, neat, dignified and proud.

And it is just that fastidiousness brought into the gutter that weighs upon me, I suppose because in acquiring this quality on our journey upward we have kinship with the cats.

They are unhappy in the presence of dirt, bad smells, and corruption. Is it perhaps that we can see ourselves, condemned by misfortune to such a life where for sustenance we might have to nose through garbage pails and offal disposal? One is never so high that one cannot be brought low, and the stray produces for us a picture of the depths.

I hear someone cry to a child, "Don't touch that cat! Can't you see it is filthy and sick?" How that beast has need of that touch denied.

And what is it that has separated the shivering bundle of misery huddled beneath a car or fleeing pell-mell over some backyard fence from the sleek and contented beast warming itself at my fireside, clean, fat, sweet-smelling, and tidy, its four feet neatly tucked beneath its shining body? Luck!

For every one of these animals upon whom luck has smiled, a thousand have been passed by and sometimes the passage was so close that only a breath, a partition of a second, a passing footfall separated it from rescue.

And so sometimes I look at my house-friend on the hearth or sitting upon my desk and think, *Do not be too proud or smug, for somewhere your counterpart is dragging itself through wretched days and nights to oblivion because Luck has passed it by, and for those hidden in the darkness beyond the lights of our windows there is no justice. Let you and me praise our Luck.*

Paul Gallico,
Honorable Cat

THE CAT THAT COULD

He was my cat, but I didn't know him very well. As a kitten he had been venturesome—the first to explore the house and go outside. That was why he was named Marco Polo, soon shortened to Marco, to which he responded, if he felt like it, with a slight twitch of an ear.

He spent most days roaming the woods back of our house. Sometimes I'd run into him there, and it would be almost like two strangers meeting, with hardly more than a glance exchanged. But he always came home to eat and sleep. So at least to that extent he was my cat.

Probably I'd not have missed Marco too much if one day he had failed to return, but something else happened. I heard the screech of car brakes and ran out to find him lying in the ditch, head thrown back, eyes wide open, unseeing.

There was no sign of life. I put him in a cardboard box, started looking for tools to dig a grave, then heard a faint moan—Marco was not dead. As best I could, I nursed him, and finally he was on his feet again, fully recovered—or so I thought. Little by little, I realized that something had happened to Marco. When we were both outside one day, I was struck by his peculiar gait, a stiff, cautious lope, each paw raised high, then thrust forward slowly. A hasty examination revealed nothing wrong that I could detect. Then as I made a sudden noise he flinched and ran—and crashed headlong into a basket left lying in the path.

He was blind.

How long had he been feeling his way like that, as a blind person taps and searches with a cane? How often had he gone hungry because he could not get past the unseen hostility of other cats to reach the food—or didn't even know the food was there? I knew that cats are usually gifted with a keen sense of smell, but when given food he was never aware of it until he walked into it. Then I thought of tapping on the floor, a signal he quickly learned meant that food had been put precisely there.

I hovered over him and snatched obstacles out of his way, until I realized that I was doing him no favor. He was still an explorer. Nothing gave him greater pleasure than discovering something out of place. So I deliberately made changes to add zest to his restricted life.

The first time I saw him on the roof, serenely sunning himself, my heart skipped a beat. Evidently sensing my presence below, he got up, yawned, and walked to the edge of the roof. He waved a paw to locate

a tree branch, tapped to make certain, then leaped, walked along the branch to the tree trunk, shinnied down, and nonchalantly ambled over to me.

As his assurance increased, so did his wandering. Soon he was visiting the woods back of the house. I'd sometimes watch with amazement as he threaded his way among the trees without ever quite bumping into anything. (Like some blind people, he seemed to have developed a kind of radar that warned him of obstacles.) Or he'd pursue windblown leaves in clumsy gallops that made me laugh and almost cry.

Only once in a while did he get lost, when the barking of a dog or some other menacing sound made him run in panic, flopping over the ground like a fish out of water, paying no attention to direction. Then he'd send out a cry that I came to recognize as a call for help.

He grew sensitive not only to my tone of voice but also to my moods. When I was out of sorts he knew it, and moped. When I was in a good mood he knew that, too, and my occasional singing, which made even me wince, delighted him so that he'd respond with a burst of gaiety, tumbling about like a playful kitten.

Era Zistel

THE KILKENNY CATS

There wanst was two cats of Kilkenny.
And aich thought there was wan cat too many;
  So they quarrelled and fit,
  And they scratched and they bit,
  Till barrin' their nails
  And the tips of their tails,
Instead of two cats, there warn't any.

Anonymous

AN APPRECIATION

I value in the cat the independent and almost ungrateful spirit which prevents her from attaching herself to any one, the indifference with which she passes from the salon to the housetop. When we caress her, she stretches herself and arches her back responsively; but this is because she feels an agreeable sensation, not because she takes a silly satisfaction, like the dog, in faithfully loving a thankless master. The cat lives alone, has no need of society, obeys only when she pleases, pretends to sleep that she may see the more clearly, and scratches everything on which she can lay her paw.

François René de Chateaubriand

CAT POSTURES

Rabbit had a wide repertoire of standard postures, and assumed them at suitable moments. A cat can put himself into more positions than a ballet dancer. Observing Rabbit, I was able to isolate a few basic ones.

First, the simplest and most typical: the Cat Couchant from which the Egyptians must have taken their model for the Sphinx. The cat lies on his stomach, four paws parallel to the ground, the front ones extended, the hind ones neatly tucked in at the sides. In a variation, the front paws are folded against the chest, mandarin style. The tail can be straight or curled around the hips, depending on the foot traffic. A good utilitarian pose for use on flat surfaces such as radiator covers, newly made beds, or even the floor.

Another posture with overtones of the ancient Egyptian is the Cat Regardant. A statuesque position, and in it the cat of the twentieth century recalls a sculpture from a thousand years ago. The seated attitude, back slightly curved, head erect, allows the cat to be at ease and alert at the same time. Good for looking out of windows on a rainy day and for general meditation. The tail, of course, must come forward until it reaches the front paws. Only an inexperienced kitten without a sense of style would let it dangle.

The Coiled Spring, or Accordion. Ideal for mouse stalking and bird watching. A wonderful demonstration of potential energy. The cat draws into himself, back strongly arched, one paw off the ground, hindquarters arched and wiggling. A vista of the jungle. Despite the evident strain, the cat can hold this pose for some time.

Also familiar is the Halloween position. Here the cat tries to imitate a crowd. The body is squeezed into the shape of an inverted "U," legs stiff, tail bristling; extremely warlike and ferocious—exactly the impression he wants to convey. Actually, he is probably scared himself and doesn't want to admit it. This is one of Rabbit's old stand-bys for use with new kittens. Effective for a while, but it doesn't take with the older hands.

I haven't mentioned the contortions involved in washing and scratching; the leg-over-elbow, 'cello-playing posture; and the doughnut, in which the cat curls up in a circle, much favored for sleeping. But a cat with ingenuity can ring changes on any of these.

Rabbit, of course, could execute them all, plus many others. But for informal relaxing at the foot of our bed, he usually lay on his side in simple elegance.

None of these positions takes into account one of the cat's most expressive features: his tail. Rabbit could point the tip of his in all directions, or crook it like an index finger. When pleased, he waved it back and forth, undulating it like the arms of a Balinese temple dancer. In anger, he gave beaver-like slaps on the floor. For inside purposes, he carried it upright, as a flagstaff; when stalking, it curved behind him like a saber.

His tail was Rabbit's regimental banner and I never knew him to lower it in defeat.

Lloyd Alexander,
My Five Tigers

THE KITTEN

A kitten is the joy of a household. All day long this incomparable actor plays his little comedy, and those who search for perpetual motion can do no better than watch his antics. His theatre is always open, any room suffices him for a stage, and he has need of few accessories. A scrap of paper, a bit of string, a spool, a pen, these are enough to incite him to marvellous acrobatic feats. . . .

Even when a kitten is quiet, he is the drollest of creatures. What a spice of innocent malice in his half-shut eyes! His head, heavy with sleep, his outstretched paws, his air of ineffable languor, all tell of comfort and content. A little drowsing cat is an image of perfect beatitude. Look at his ears. How big and comical they are. No sound, however faint, escapes them. Look at his eyes when he opens them wide. How quick and keen their glance. Who is that knocking? Who is that crossing the room? What is there good to eat in box, or bundle, or basket? The ruling passion of a kitten is curiosity, and in this regard he is uncommonly like a child. "When a cat enters a room for the first time," says Rousseau in *Emile*, "he prowls into every corner, he cannot rest until he has made himself familiar with his surroundings. So does a young child behave when he is beginning to walk and talk. So does he question the unknown world he is entering."

There is no more intrepid explorer than a kitten. He makes perilous voyages into cellar and attic, he scales the roofs of neighbouring houses, he thrusts his little inquiring nose into half-shut doors, he lays up for future use a store of useful observation, he gets himself into every kind of trouble, and is always sorry when it is too late. It is amazing to see a kitten climb a tree. Up he goes from bough to bough, higher and higher, as though bent on enjoying the view from the top. He does not ask where this delightful adventure is taking him. He pays no heed to the diminishing size of the branches, and it is only when they sway beneath his weight that he realizes the impossibility of mounting any further. Then fear grips his heart, and he mews appealingly for help. Somebody must hasten with a ladder to his rescue; and, until aid comes, he slides pitifully and perilously along an upper branch, clawing it with desperate precautions. His heart, we know, is beating as though it would break, his agility has deserted him, his audacity has given way to despair.

Jules Husson Champfleury

70

THE COMPANIONABLE CAT

My cat in winter time usually sleeps upon my dog, who submits in patience; and I have often found her on horseback in the stable, not from any taste for equestrianism, but simply because a horsecloth is a perpetual warmer when there is a living horse beneath it. She loves the dog and horse with the tender regard we have for foot-warmers and railway rugs during a journey in the depth of winter; nor have I ever been able to detect in her any worthier sentiment towards her master. Yet of all animals that we can have in a room with us, the cat is the least disquieting. Her presence is soothing to a student, as the presence of a quiet nurse is soothing to an invalid. It is agreeable to feel that you are not absolutely alone, and it seems to you, when you are at work, as if the cat took care that all her movements should be noiseless, purely out of consideration for your comfort. Then, if you have time to caress her, you know that she will purr a response, and why inquire too closely into the sincerity of her affection?

Philip Gilbert Hamerton

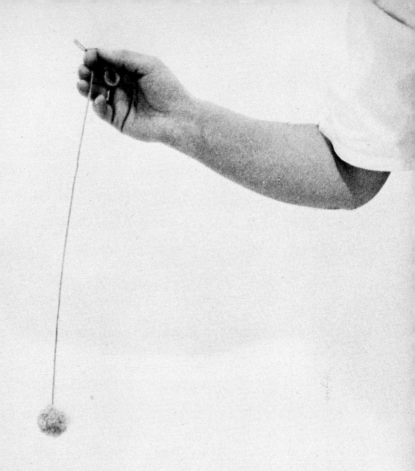

WHEN I PLAY WITH MY CAT

When I play with my cat
who knows whether I do
not make her more sport
than she makes me?

Michel de Montaigne

THE RETIRED CAT

A Poet's Cat, sedate and grave
As poet well could wish to have,
Was much addicted to inquire
For nooks to which she might retire,
And where, secure as mouse in chink,
She might repose, or sit and think.
I know not where she caught the trick;
Nature perhaps herself had cast her
In such a mold PHILOSOPHIC,
Or else she learned it of her master.
Sometimes ascending, debonair,
An apple tree or lofty pear,
Lodged with convenience in the fork,
She watched the gardener at his work;
Sometimes her ease and solace sought
In an old empty watering-pot,
There wanting nothing save a fan
To seem some nymph in her sedan,
Appareled in exactest sort,
And ready to be borne to court.

But love of change it seems has place
Not only in our wiser race;
Cats also feel as well as we
That passion's force, and so did she.
Her climbing, she began to find,
Exposed her too much to the wind,
And the old utensil of tin
Was cold and comfortless within;
She therefore wished, instead of those,
Some place of more serene repose,

Where neither cold might come, nor air
Too rudely wanton in her hair,
And sought it in the likeliest mode
Within her master's snug abode.

A drawer, it chanced, at bottom lined,
With linen of the softest kind,
With such as merchants introduce
From India, for the ladies' use;
A drawer, impending o'er the rest,
Half open, in the topmost chest,
Of depth enough and none to spare,
Invited her to slumber there;
Puss with delight beyond expression,
Surveyed the scene and took possession.
Recumbent at her ease, ere long,
And lulled by her own humdrum song,
She left the cares of life behind,
And slept as she would sleep her last,
When in came, housewifely inclined,
The chambermaid, and shut it fast,
By no malignity impelled,
But all unconscious whom it held.
Awakened by the shock (cried Puss),
"Was ever cat attended thus!
The open drawer was left, I see,
Merely to prove a nest for me,

For soon as I was well composed,
Then came the maid, and it was closed.
How smooth those 'kerchiefs and how sweet,
Oh, what a delicate retreat!
I will resign myself to rest
Till Sol declining in the West,
Shall call to supper, when no doubt,
Susan will come and let me out."

The evening came, the sun descended,
And Puss remained, still unattended.
The night rolled tardily away
(With her, indeed, 'twas never day),
The sprightly morn her course renewed,
The evening gray again ensued,
And Puss came into mind no more
Than if entombed the day before;
With hunger pinched and pinched for room,
She now presaged approaching doom.
Nor slept a single wink, nor purred,
Conscious of jeopardy incurred.

That night, by chance, the poet, watching,
Heard an inexplicable scratching;
His noble heart went pit-a-pat,
And to himself he said, "What's that?"
He drew the curtain at his side,
And forth he peeped, but nothing spied.
Yet by his ear directed, guessed
Something imprisoned in the chest;
And doubtful what, with prudent care
Resolved it should continue there.
At length a voice, which well he knew
A long and melancholy mew,
Saluting his poetic ears,
Consoled him and dispelled his fears;
He left his bed, he trod the floor,
He 'gan in haste the drawers explore,
The lowest first, and without stop
The next in order to the top.

For 'tis a truth well known to most,
That whatsoever thing is lost,
We seek it, ere it come to light,
In every cranny but the right.
Forth skipped the cat, not now replete
As erst with airy self-conceit,
Nor in her own fond comprehension,
A theme for all the world's attention,
But modest, sober, cured of all
Her notions hyperbolical
And wishing for a place of rest,
Anything rather than a chest.
Then stepped the poet into bed
With this reflection in his head:

Moral

Beward of too sublime a sense
Of your own worth and consequence.
The man who dreams himself so great,
And his importance of such weight,
That all around in all that's done,
Must move and act for him alone,
Will learn in school of tribulation
The folly of his expectation.

William Cowper

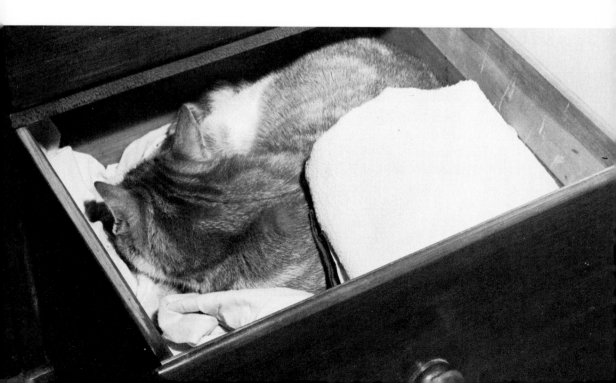

MY CAT JEOFFRY

For I will consider my Cat Jeoffry.

For he is the servant of the Living God, duly and daily serving him.

For at the first glance of the glory of God in the East he worships in his way.

For is this done by wreathing his body seven times round with elegant quickness.

For then he leaps up to catch the musk, [which] is the blessing of God upon his prayer.

For he rolls upon prank to work it in.

For having done duty and received blessing he begins to consider himself.

For this he performs in ten degrees.

For first he looks upon his fore-paws to see if they are clean.

For secondly he kicks up behind to clear away there.

For thirdly he works it upon stretch with the forepaws extended.

For fourthly he sharpens his paws by wood.

For fifthly he washes himself.

For sixthly he rolls upon wash.

For seventhly he fleas himself, that he may not be interrupted upon the beat.

For eighthly he rubs himself against a post.

For ninthly he looks up for his instructions.

For tenthly he goes in quest of food.

For having consider'd God and himself he will consider his neighbour.

For if he meets another cat he will kiss her in kindness.

For when he takes his prey he plays with it to give it [a] chance.

For one mouse in seven escapes by his dallying.

For when his day's work is done his business more properly begins.

For he keeps the Lord's watch in the night against the adversary.

For he counteracts the powers of darkness by his electrical skin & glaring eyes.

For he counteracts the Devil, who is death, by brisking about the life.

For in his morning orisons he loves the sun and the sun loves him.

For he is of the tribe of Tiger.

For the Cherub Cat is a term of the Angel Tiger.

For he has the subtlety and hissing of a serpent, which in goodness he suppresses.

For he will not do destruction, if he is well-fed, neither will he spit without provocation.

For he purrs in thankfulness, when God tells him he's a good Cat.

For he is an instrument for the children to learn benevolence upon.

For every house is incompleat without him & a blessing is lacking in the spirit.

Christopher Smart,
Rejoice in the Lamb

PLAYING WITH A CAT

A famous nineteenth-century singing teacher's first advice to a pupil was always: "No one can learn to sing until he has learned not to be afraid of looking a fool." Remembering a Siamese whose favourite game was to be stalked on hands and knees in dead silence round the drawing-room furniture and through the house until she collapsed from the pure ecstasy of her excitement, I feel the same might be said of playing with cats.

If you are self-conscious, it is best done when you are alone with the cat for provided you play the right game fairly, the cat will not think you look a fool. It is only if you allow your concentration to falter or break the rules that the cat will break off with a "if-you're-amused-I'm-not" twitch of the tail.

Playing with a cat—or allowing a cat to play with you—can be fascinating and relaxing as many great men burdened with affairs of state have found, from Louis XIII's cardinal-minister Richelieu to Sir Winston Churchill. But it is a pastime that requires study and time to yield the fullest enjoyment. Those who think that playing with a cat means nothing but dangling a piece of string deny themselves pleasure. The game is likely to end with the human player muttering "Dull cat" because he has failed to match the cat's imagination with his own. It takes two to play "Let's pretend," even though neither is genuinely deceived and the ability to play successfully with a cat, even more than with a young child, is an exercise in imagination for it demands entering the world of a very different creature.

Games with cats are unlike any others, except perhaps with individual children. Although all cat games have their rules and ritual, these vary with each individual player. There is no game that appeals to all cats at all times and probably no cat which, given opportunity, will not invent its own unique game. These highly individual games develop rules as formal and refined as those of cricket and football. Any

breach of the rules on the part of the human player is likely to bring the game to an abrupt end. The cat, of course, never breaks a rule. If it does not follow precedent, that simply means it has created a new rule and it is up to you to learn it quickly if you want the game to continue.

But the cat is such an individualist that all generalizations are likely to prove false with particular cats. I have in mind a cat who developed a complicated game, the basis of which was somersaulting from a concealed position on to a feather. When she felt lazy or perhaps thought that the game was not going sufficiently in her favour, she would "cheat" by taking up an advanced position. But a stern warning that you would not play if she did not go to her place always resulted in a retreat, even if it were accompanied by tail-lashing and verbal protests that would have done credit to a footballer addressing the referee after being whistled for a foul.

Inventing games requires observation of the nature of cats in general and one cat in particular. All cats, for instance, are more interested by the movement of an object they cannot see than one which is visible. A mysterious rustle in a bush is worth two wiggles of a string on the path beside it. Pouncing from a hiding place is instinctive in all cats. So is jumping. There are endless games that can be based on these facts. But it is axiomatic that you cannot order a cat to play. You can only coax or beguile.

"Performing" is rather different from playing, but if the tricks the cat is persuaded to perform are in keeping with its physical and mental characteristics, it may enjoy them, whether it is jumping over a door or walking along a tightrope. Many cats take easily to retrieving, provided the size and texture of the object is suitable. A rabbit's foot is ideal. I had one cat who would retrieve her rabbit's foot from down two flights of stairs again and again until exhaustion set in—mine, not hers, for once she asked for a game, she was tireless.

When we moved to another house, she gave up the game. It was something that belonged to a certain place and time and had no meaning anywhere else. This ritualism seems characteristic of cats. A game favoured at twilight, when offered at midday seems as ridiculous as football in June. A rabbit's foot thrown across the floor is treated with contempt if the rules of the game demand it be thrown downstairs.

The most fascinating of cat games are the improbable ones. Sir William Nicholson . . . had a cat of his own called Black, whose games included being spun in a very large wooden bowl. He would get into the bowl, acquired for a still-life painting, and demand that it should be spun at an ever increasing speed. He nestled in this miniature "wall of death" until the human player was tired, when, staggering slightly and purring like a marathon runner who has just broken the record, he would make for his favourite seat. Such a sensation would certainly terrify most cats and it is this discovery of the one unique game that each individual cat desires which represents a challenge to the cat-lover with a taste for playing.

Going for a walk is perhaps hardly a game, but most cats enjoy it if encouraged. The encouragement calls for no more than suiting the walk to the cat and understanding that cats do not go for a walk to get somewhere but to explore and that their senses are so acute that even if the walk is made twice daily on the same route, each time is a fresh exploration. In contrast to a dog, a cat progresses by starts and stops, with continual pauses and diversions too feline for a human being to understand, although he may get pleasure from trying to do so.

Apart from pleasure, playing with a cat is good for it. Many cats, especially in towns, have insufficient opportunities for exercise. The pouncing, leaping, rolling and running demanded by games prevent middle-aged spread, with benefit to the spirit as well as appearance. A much-played-with cat remains a playful cat far into old age.

Sidney Denham,
Our Cats

FACIAL EXPRESSIONS

The cat's large variety of facial expressions is not equaled by those of any other animal save man. They convey pleasure, amusement, pain, perplexity, mischief, fright, interrogation, expectancy, triumph, grief, and other emotions. Cats frown when annoyed and sometimes assume a sweet expression when talked to. A cat will put on a very sweet face when a loved child picks it up, and the expression of the female generally is somewhat softer than that of the male. The face is a certain guide to the manner of life of the cat and instantly reveals the character of its home, particularly in the expression of the eyes, the glance of the well-treated cat being mild and trustful, while that of the ill-used cat is hard and suspicious.

Ida M. Mellen,
The Science and the Mystery of the Cat

CATS AS MOTHERS

Amongst domestic animals, cats are by far the most ardent and skilled mothers. The word "blissful" always suggests to me the expression of a cat who has given birth to her kittens, cleaned them up and settled to suckle them, an expression made from equal parts of sensual pleasure, pride and contentment that she has fulfilled herself.

The immense satisfaction a cat finds in motherhood is embodied in the crooning sound which she makes only when speaking to her kittens, graphically described by Karel Capek as "not a note, but a whole chord in harmonic thirds and fifths, very similar to the chord on a mouth organ."

The strength of the maternal urge and the devotion of a cat to her kittens is one of the reasons for the survival of the species and its world-wide distribution in spite of periods of neglect and even persecution. The courage and fierceness of a cat with kittens is too well known to need emphasis. The wild cat that killed an armed knight at Barnborough in Yorkshire in the Middle Ages was perhaps protecting her kittens in the forest. Although she died of her wounds, her kittens probably survived.

There are well-authenticated instances of cats jumping into rivers and entering burning houses to save their kittens. And a cat continually deprived of her kittens will often make sure of the next litter's survival by giving birth to it in some hidden and inaccessible spot.

Although domesticated for several thousand years, the instincts of the wild animal remain unimpaired in the cat and some of them can be seen at work in completely changed conditions during maternity. After the birth of her kittens, a mother cleans up scrupulously. She may be on a blanket in a basket in a secure home, but promptings from her prehistoric past urge her to leave no trace that would enable her enemies to track her lair when she leaves her kittens defenceless to hunt for food for herself so that she can feed them.

A cat with kittens nearly always decides sooner or later to move them. However comfortable she may be, she decides they would be better somewhere else. There follows the search for some usually quite unsuitable cupboard or shelf in another room and the skilful carrying of the kittens. She is not to be denied and can become the despair of a fond owner who cannot imagine what is wrong with the box or basket provided.

What can be the explanation but that in the mind of the cat the basket is a small cave or hole or even a nest in long grass, as it was five thousand years ago, and that after coming and going for several days, she has made a trail which would guide her enemies to it? So the insistence on the move, even though now there are no enemies, and the trail on the carpet is invisible. Once decided on, nothing will stop the move.

Sidney Denham,
Our Cats

MENTU

The wild nature in Mentu is as strong as his inbred civilization; and the two are at strife together. His heart and his appetite lead him back and back to the house; keep him there for days together, a dainty fine gentleman, warm-hearted, capricious. But the spirit of the wild creature rises in him, and the night comes when, at bedtime, no Mentu is waiting at the door to be let in; or in the evening, as he hears the wind rise and stir the branches, even while the rain beats on the window pane, the compelling power of out-of-doors is on him, and he must go; and when the window is lifted, and the night air streams in, there is but one leap into the darkness.

He will return early in the morning, tired and satiate, or spring in some evening as the dusk gathers, with gleaming eyes where the light of the wild woods flickers and dies down in the comfortable firelight of an English home.

This is the true cat, the real Mentu, this wild creature who must go on his mysterious errands; or who, I rather believe it, plunges out to revel in the intoxication of innumerable scents, unaccounted sounds, and the half-revealed forms of wood and field in twilight, in darkness, or in dawn. In his soul he is a dramatist, an artist in sensation. He lives with human beings, he loves them, as we live with children and love them, and play their games. But the great world calls us, and we must go; and Mentu's business in life is elsewhere. He lives in the half-lights, in secret places, free and alone,—this mysterious little-great being whom his mistress calls "My cat."

Margaret Benson,
The Soul of a Cat

A POET'S KITTEN

I have a kitten, my dear, the drollest of all creatures that ever wore a cat's skin. Her gambols are incredible, and not to be described. She tumbles head over heels several times together. She lays her cheek to the ground, and humps her back at you with an air of most supreme disdain. From this posture she rises to dance on her hind feet, an exercise which she performs with all the grace imaginable; and she closes these various exhibitions with a loud smack of her lips, which, for want of greater propriety of expression, we call spitting. But, though all cats spit, no cat ever produced such a sound as she does. In point of size, she is likely to be a kitten always, being extremely small for her age; but time, that spoils all things, will, I suppose, make her also a cat. You will see her, I hope, before that melancholy period shall arrive; for no wisdom that she may gain by experience and reflection hereafter will compensate for the loss of her present hilarity.

William Cowper

PECUNIARY CANONS OF TASTE

Barnyard fowl, hogs, cattle, sheep, goats, draught-horses . . . are of the nature of productive goods, and serve a useful, often a lucrative end; therefore beauty is not readily imputed to them. The case is different with those domestic animals which ordinarily serve no industrial end; such as pigeons, parrots and other cage-birds, cats, dogs, and fast horses. These commonly are items of conspicuous consumption, and are therefore honorific in their nature and may legitimately be accounted beautiful. . . .

Apart from the birds which belong in the honorific class of domestic animals, and which owe their place in this class to their non-lucrative character alone, the animals which merit particular attention are cats, dogs, and fast horses. The cat is less reputable than the other two just named because she is less wasteful; she may even serve a useful end. At the same time the cat's temperament does not fit her for the honorific purpose. She lives with man on terms of equality, knows nothing of that relation of status which is the ancient basis of all distinctions of worth, honour, and repute, and she does not lend herself with facility to an invidious comparison between her owner and his neighbours. The exception to this last rule occurs in the case of such scarce and fanciful products as the Angora cat, which have some slight honorific value on the ground of expensiveness, and have, therefore, some special claim to beauty on pecuniary grounds.

Thorstein Veblen
The Theory of the Leisure Class

THE MODERN CAT

With the possible exception of the cow, the cat seems to the unsophis-
ticated eye to be, of all domestic animals, the one who has most opportunity for mental activity. She wastes no time bidding for our attention
or bewailing our neglect as does the dog; she performs no time-consum-
ing labours as does the horse; she lacks to our eyes, moreover, the appearance of feeble-mindedness which distinguishes the pig, or the
preoccupation with alimentation for which the sheep and chickens are
notable. You find her curled by the hour in front of the fire, or sitting
all day long by the mouse hole, or on the mantelshelf looking down, or
under the porch looking up. What is she doing? The simplest answer
seems to many to be: "She just sits and thinks."

By providing herself thus with opportunity for contemplation the
cat seems to have arranged her life in a most intelligent though possibly
unethical way. She is like the lady of fashion who so directs her affairs
that all necessary work shall be performed by some one else and her
own time left free for pleasure. The cat gives the world nothing and re-
ceives from it everything. Like the goldfish she provides us with neither shelter, food, nor clothing (for "cat fur" though warm and pretty is
for some reason socially taboo). But unlike the simple fish she suffers
no curtailment of her freedom. Like the dog, she gains sufficient exercise in her own way and at her own time. But a blade of grass or a curtain tassel provides a much more accessible playfellow than a human
being willing to whistle or throw sticks. And in spite of a life of relative
freedom from care for food and shelter, her instinctive equipment remains such that if occasion arises, as when she is abandoned perhaps in
the woods, she is much better fitted to resume a wild life than is the
dog. But usually you find her in our homes. There she occupies a position much like that accorded by primitive theology to the deity. Her
function is to sit and be admired.

Georgina Stickland Gates,
The Modern Cat: Her Mind and Manners

THE MYSTERIOUS CAT

I saw a proud, mysterious cat,
I saw a proud, mysterious cat,
Too proud to catch a mouse or rat—
Mew, mew, mew.

But catnip she would eat, and purr,
But catnip she would eat, and purr.
And goldfish she did much prefer—
Mew, mew, mew.

I saw a cat—'twas but a dream,
I saw a cat—'twas but a dream,
Who scorned the slave that brought her cream—
Mew, mew, mew.

Unless the slave were dressed in style,
Unless the slave were dressed in style,
And knelt before her all the while—
Mew, mew, mew.

Did you ever hear of a thing like that?
Did you ever hear of a thing like that?
Oh, what a proud, mysterious cat.
Oh, what a proud, mysterious cat.
Oh, what a proud, mysterious cat.
Mew . . . mew . . . mew.

Vachel Lindsay,
Johnny Appleseed and Other Poems

CURIOSITY

Another visible manifestation of the cat's elaborate defense mechanism is its overwhelming curiosity. Think a minute! Observe a cat making its meticulous survey of the bags from the supermarket, the gift packages under the Christmas tree, the birthday or anniversary goodies, visitor's luggage, the delivery cartons, the new dried arrangement or floral centerpiece on the dining room table . . . everything of any size, shape, or description introduced into the cat's environment must undergo minute examination. Why? It is foreign to the cat's nature to be surprised. It either angers or intimidates.

The inspection routine is the animal classification method. The built-in cat cat computer prints it out this way: Animate things—I'll retreat and watch; inanimate—I'll forget this one; it could become part of the scenery—possible enemy; I'll either stand and fight or run and hide.

Bill Adams

CANINE VS. FELINE

Psychologists and researchers generally agree that dogs are smarter than cats, but cat lovers often wonder on what basis this conclusion was made. Psychologists cite experiments with albino rats, with hooded rats; they overwhelm us with words we've never heard before—like statistical analysis, standard deviation, affect, instinctual drift, Skinner Box, and many others. Then, when it comes to the intelligence of cats, they always conclude that "dogs are smarter."

I for one cannot agree, but then, I don't have a master's degree in psychology. On the other hand, I do have the experience, thirty years of it. Brought up in a home where felines were defamed, called two-faced and vicious, and where man's best friend was placed on the proverbial pedestal, I was taken aback when my bride brought cats (as well as the love for the feline) into our home immediately after the wedding. Without asking. Thus, I learned about cats. More than I ever expected to learn, I dare say.

When you ask a psychologist why dogs are considered smarter, they'll say it's "because they learn faster." Although this appears to be true, it certainly is not the whole story.

Here I have to detour a bit. Recently an interesting chap named Dr. Peter wrote a book in which he described—in great detail—what he called "the Peter Principle." It's about how everyone eventually arrives at his level of incompetence. To prevent this from happening to those who do not want to perform at such a level, he gives specific instructions on how to avoid promotions.

I submit that prehistoric cats had their own Dr. Peter. I can see it quite clearly: "OK, you cats, if you want to be smart—smarter than those clumsy, slobbering dogs—you gotta play it cool." And he proceeded to program them accordingly.

Item: It's the dog that brings in the newspaper on a cold day and fetches the slippers, while kitty snoozes in front of the fireplace. It's the

dog that wears himself out fetching this or that, doing one or another trick and making up to everyone, friend or foe alike.

Item: Most people don't know it, but cats are expert swimmers. Cats pretend to hate water. Just splash a few drops onto their immaculate fur and they'll take off like an overfueled rocket. (Let the dumb dogs get wet and stringy when they try to fetch the sticks playful humans throw into polluted rivers and lakes! Us cats take a bath when *we* want to.) The charming gray male kitten we recently gave away to an attractive young lady friend regularly takes a bath with her—at his own choosing of time, place, and condition. (He swims beautifully.)

Item: Our sixteen-year-old Siamese, Koko, at times is not willing to come into the house when we are ready to retire. Tough luck! We go to bed. In the morning, Koko is let in. What would a dog do in this case? He'd lick your hand and slobber all over you. He is so happy to see you and grateful that you condescend to let him in. Koko, on the other hand, lets you know in no uncertain terms that you are an inconsiderate heel and a racist who does not care about minorities. He bawls you out unmercifully as he marches up to his food dish to garbage up, and he still squawks at you after he's had his fill and climbs into his basket for his so cruelly delayed slumber.

Item: Last month, our neighbor's house turned into a disaster area for a whole week. Red, their long-haired Irish Setter had let his enthusiasm to befriend a passing skunk get the better of him. When our Koko encountered the same animal the following day, he sat down at a safe distance and the two animals contemplated each other with mutual respect for a long time, while we anxiously watched them through the window. We breathed deep sighs of relief when we realized that Koko's superior judgment had preserved the tranquility of his world—*our home!*

Item: Dogs eat sloppily, noisily, indiscriminately, and carelessly: Stones, poison, food, bones—it's all the same to them. Cats sniff at every bite. Dogs overeat, cats know when to stop. Dogs get themselves filthy and require repeated—and hated—baths. Cats keep themselves dainty and clean. Dogs get angry when left alone and wreck the house; cats know better. Dogs have to be housebroken, but cats demonstrate their superior toilet habits right from birth.

Item: You can beat a dog and he will still love you. But beat a cat (that is if you can catch him) and you'll either wind up with crimson streaks, or he will ignore you—showing not only that you rate less than zero in his book, but also that you'll never get anywhere that way.

And what was the sage advice the early feline Dr. Peter instilled in his race? Simply this: *The smart cat doesn't let on that he is.*

H. G. Frommer

FALLING CAT

I remember as a child watching a cat leaping playfully from one window ledge to another on the fourth story of a building above a stone pavement. She slipped and fell. I was terrified. A drop of that distance would have killed a man. But the cat jumped right up, seemed a bit disconcerted, and ran away as though frightened. She had landed on her feet!

The cat is able, when she falls, to turn in the air and land squarely on her feet. She has been photographed during the process and investigators have studied not only the mechanics of the reflex, but also the extent of her ability and the sense organs on which it probably depends.

The rotation in the air will occur to one side or the other, depending upon the animal's initial position. If she is held with her back down, her legs inclining to the right, she will turn to that side; if the legs originally point more to the left, the rotation will be in that direction. Motion pictures show that the animal first contracts her fore legs and then turns her fore part around. This makes the hind part turn in the opposite direction but to a less extent. Then she contracts her hind legs, extends the fore legs and gives the hind part a turn. This turns the fore legs a little again in the opposite direction, but again slightly. The cat can turn herself through any angle by continuing contractions of this kind.

Some cats were held by an investigator in a horizontal position with their backs to the floor, then dropped from varying distances on a soft bed of straw. (The bed of straw was provided by a thoughtful experimenter who was not certain of his subjects' prowess.) The cats invariably made the rotation as soon as support was removed. All were able to turn perfectly even when the distance of the fall was only one foot! Some were able to turn in six inches.

Even when unable to see, the cat's reactions were about as perfect

and as quick, though their landing on the straw was not so accurate for they were ignorant as to the height of the fall. Even when the organs within the ear (the semi-circular canals) which give both man and animals a perception of the rotation of their bodies, were not functioning, the cats were still capable of turning. Only when sensations from both eyesight and the sense of equilibrium were cut off were they unable to react. Probably the normal cat depends both on vision and the sense of equilibrium for her cues in performing the falling reflex. It seems also probable that the turning depends on the presence of consciousness and that the unconscious animal does not so react.

Georgina Stickland Gates,
The Modern Cat: Her Mind and Manners

103

A CAT NAMED SLOOPY

For a while
the only earth that Sloopy knew
                was in her sandbox.
   Two rooms on Fifty-fifth Street
            were her domain.
Every night she'd sit in the window
among the avocado plants
waiting for me to come home
      (my arms full of canned liver and love).
We'd talk into the night then
                  contented
but missing something.
She the earth she never knew
me the hills I ran
            while growing bent.

Sloopy should have been a cowboy's cat
with prairies to run
                not linoleum
and real-live catnip mice.
No one to depend on but herself.

I never told her
   but in my mind
I was a midnight cowboy even then.
Riding my imaginary horse
down Forty-second Street,
going off with strangers
to live an hour-long cowboy's life,
         but always coming home to Sloopy,
      who loved me best. . . .

Rod McKuen,
Listen to the Warm

CATS TRAIN THEIR KITTENS

Cats train their kittens
just how to fend for themselves,
and then throw them out.

Louise Lessin,
Cats and Their People in Haiku

DRAWING THE CAT

Makes a platform for himself:
forepaws bent under his chest,
slot-eyes shut in a corniced head,
haunches high like a wing chair,
hindlegs parallel, a sled.

As if on water, low afloat
like a wooden duck: a bundle not
apt to be tipped, so symmetrized
on hidden keel of tail he rides
squat, arrested, glazed.

Lying flat, a violin:
hips are splayed, head and chin
sunk on paws, stem straight out
from the arched root
at the clef-curve of the thighs.

Wakes: the head rises.
Claws sprawl. Wires
go taut, make a wicket of his spine.
He humps erect, with scimitar yawn
of hooks and needles porcupine.

Sits, solid as a doorstop,
tail-encircled, tip laid on his toes,
ear-tabs stiff, gooseberry eyes
full, unblinking, sourly wise.
In outline: a demijohn with a pewter look.

Swivels, bends a muscled neck:
petal-of-tulip-tongue slicks
the brushpoint of his tail to black,
then smooths each glossy epaulette
with assiduous sponge.

Whistle him into a canter
into the kitchen: tail hooked aside,
ears at the ready. Elegant copy
of carrousel pony—
eyes bright as money.

May Swenson,
Half Sun Half Sleep

CATS

Cats sleep
Anywhere,
Any table,
Any chair,
Top of piano,
Window-ledge,
In the middle,
On the edge,
Open drawer,
Empty shoe,
Anybody's
Lap will do,
Fitted in a
Cardboard box,
In the cupboard
With your frocks—
Anywhere!
They don't care!
Cats sleep
Anywhere.

Eleanor Farjeon,
The Children's Bells

VERSES ON A CAT

A cat in distress,
Nothing more, nor less;
Good Folks, I must faithfully tell ye,
As I am a sinner,
It waits for some dinner
To stuff out its own little belly.

You would not easily guess
All the modes of distress
Which torture the tenants of earth;
And the various evils,
Which like so many devils,
Attend the poor souls from their birth.

Some a living require,
And others desire
An old fellow out of the way;
And which is the best
I leave to be guessed,
For I cannot pretend to say.

One wants society,
Another variety,
Others a tranquil life;
Some want food.
Others, as good,
Only want a wife.

But this poor little cat
Only wanted a rat,
To stuff out its own little maw;
And it were as good
Some people had such food,
To make them hold their jaw.

Percy Bysshe Shelley

THE HYPOCRISY OF CATS?

The hypocrisy of cats? This is more than anthropological slander; it is calumny, current just because our judgment too often requires forced demonstrations. But the cat is utterly sincere. "In cats," said Louis Pergaud, who was well acquainted with the species, "a straightening of the eyebrows, a laying back of the ears, the bristling of the whiskers, or puckering of the nose, an imperceptible wrinkling of the lip, the extending or contraction of the eyelids, the lashing of the tail, and certain ways of hunching up and putting their weight on one paw, are precursory signs of the storm, and are scarcely ever misleading."

How better could they send out a warning? They could hardly use words more eloquently to express their anger. A hypocrite is someone who smiles, flatters, and detests you, protesting his friendship the better to betray you afterward. Perhaps you may prefer to the cat's way the crafty air with which certain watchdogs will approach you on the sly and seize hold of your coattails if you make the least move away.

When the cat explodes in a fury, there is thunder and lightning at once, the light of murder in his eyes; and it is impossible to suppress or calm the storm. In fact, one's obstinacy or clumsiness in trying to abate it will often aggravate it. Surely this is anything but hypocritical. It is a faithful, accurate explanation of the explosive behavior of an animal who is incapable of hiding his feelings, and who can never be brought to suppress them.

Fernand Méry,
Her Majesty the Cat

CATS' GIFTS

Cats have many gifts that are denied humans, and yet we tend to rate them by human standards. To understand a cat, you must realize that he has his own gifts, his own viewpoint, even his own morality. A cat's lack of speech does not make him a lower animal. Cats have a contempt of speech. Why should they talk when they can communicate without words? They manage very well among themselves, and they patiently try to make their thoughts known to humans. But in order to read a cat, you must be relaxed and receptive.

Lilian Jackson Braun,
The Cat Who Could Read Backwards

VIGILANT AS A CAT

I am as vigilant as a cat to steal cream.

William Shakespeare,
Henry IV

119

AN HUMBLE PETITION PRESENTED
TO MADAME HELVE'TIUS BY HER CATS

We shall not endeavour to defend ourselves equally from devouring as many sparrows, blackbirds, and thrushes, as we can possibly catch. But here we have to plead in extenuation, that our most cruel enemies, your Abbés themselves, are incessantly complaining of the ravages made by these birds among the cherries and other fruit. The Sieur Abbé Morellet, in particular, is always thundering the most violent anathemas against the blackbirds and thrushes, for plundering your vines, which they do with as little mercy as he himself. To us, however, most illustrious Lady, it appears that the grapes may just as well be eaten by *blackbirds* as by *Abbés*, and that our warfare against the winged plunderers will be fruitless, if you encourage other biped and featherless pilferers, who make ten times more havoc.

We know that we are also accused of eating nightingales, who never plunder, and sing, as they say, most enchantingly. It is indeed possible that we may now and then have gratified our palates with a delicious morsel in this way, but we can assure you that it was in utter ignorance of your affection for the species; and that, resembling sparrows in their plumage, we, who make no pretensions to being connoisseurs in music, could not distinguish the song of the one from that of the other, and therefore supposed ourselves regaling only on sparrows. A cat belonging to M. Piccini has assured us, that they who only know how to *mew*, cannot be any judges of the art of singing; and on this we rest for our justification. However, we will henceforward exert our utmost endeavours to distinguish the *Gluckists*, who are, as we are informed, the sparrows, from the *Piccinists*, who are the nightingales. We only intreat of you to pardon the inadvertence into which we may possibly fall, if, in roving after nests, we may sometimes fall upon a brood of *Piccinists*, who, being then destitute of plumage, and not having learnt to sing, will have no mark by which to distinguish them.

Benjamin Franklin,
Franklin's Wit and Folly

121

CAT VS. DOG

Living with a kitten or cat is a rewarding experience. Like dogs, they ask so little and give so much. And they still carry within themselves so many traits that have come down from the ancient past.

Man has had for thousands of years what the biologists call a symbiotic relationship with certain other species, which means that both live together for their mutual benefit. It is not exactly fair because we are always at the top and the animal has to adjust to us. We have seldom, if ever, tried to maintain this symbiosis on a fair basis.

We began the association for our own uses. Dogs could chase the primitive hunter's prey and bring it in and receive a bone for reward. Cats could keep down the rat and mouse population, not to mention moles and other small predators, and in return get a few inches by the fire to curl up in.

We had the best of both worlds, using the skill of our symbiotic associates but feeling no responsibility in return. Now we are supposed to be highly civilized creatures, although we alone deliberately kill our own kind, the lower animals do not—except perhaps in the heat of sexual competition.

In the long history of mankind, dogs have been easiest to subjugate. A dog will put up with almost anything. Dogs have infinite patience with this peculiar breed that controls their destinies and will even wear skirts and headdresses and run around on their hind legs to amuse people.

Cats, on the other hand, have managed to keep a kind of independence. They are determined to preserve a little of their original personality. This is the reason so many people say they would never have a cat because a cat is unmanageable. As one who loves and admires both dogs and cats, I may say this is exceedingly silly. We do not expect everyone to be exactly alike, and if we feel a cat should be like a dog, we are missing something important.

Gladys Taber,
Amber, a Very Personal Cat

122

QUALITIES OF CATS

With the qualities of cleanliness, discretion, affection, patience, dignity, and courage that cats have, how many of us, I ask you, would be capable of being cats?

Fernand Méry,
Her Majesty the Cat

CATS' EYES

There are several things about cats that, in primitive minds, are sufficient to connect them with the moon. First, of course, are their eyes which have such a strange and beautiful luminosity and a seemingly weird ability to penetrate the dark. Men fear the dark and cats do not, which is enough to suggest that the cat has some sort of understanding with whatever power rules the world of night. A she-cat suckling kittens lies in a suggestive crescent and is the very essence of maternity. The moon has often been connected with fertility, amorous passion and the female principle, and all of these are very evident properties of the cat.

The way cats walk noiselessly and leap, as carelessly as though an unseen hand were guiding them, to some high place was enough to put the hair up on many a primitive human. Cats do other things which can be taken as signs that they see, hear and know things imperceptible to human beings. The conformation of the cat's eye gives it a clear yet shallow stare which strikes humans as inscrutable. Its gaze is intense, and yet it is sometimes hard to see just what the cat is looking at, and consequently easy to imagine that it is seeing the unseeable.

Cats have a habit of concentrating when there is apparently nothing to concentrate on, and at other times seem suddenly to respond, with quick attention or an unaccountable leap, to something that isn't there. In other words, they seem to see ghosts. Sometimes a cat's fur crackles with electricity when it is stroked, giving an eerie tingling to the fingers of the stroker, or it may even make tiny visible sparks. This may presage a change in weather, suggesting that the cat had something to do with events in the future. Even the general behavior of cats, so independent of anything but inner dictates, can make it seem as though the cat received guidance from any uncanny source. Sometimes this behavior is connected with a specific event so it appears, by hindsight, that the cat must have been gifted with foresight.

Faith McNulty and Elizabeth Keiffer,
Wholly Cats

CATS AND HUMANS—ALL THE SAME

Of all the beasts that live, we must,
I guess, call Cats the humanust;
For jest like folks, you'll find that these
Has no end to their qualities.
For some is fat and some is lean,
Some very dirty and some clean,—
Some's always licken at their fur
And some's not so particular.
Some Cats take jest fresh milk and meat,
Some takes all that they're gave to eat.
Some Cats they cough, and some they wheeze,
And some's afflicted by dizeeze;
Some Cats is blind, and stone-deaf some,
But aint no Cat wuz ever dumb.
Some Cats will monkey round and fool,
And play for hours with jest a spool,
While some jest sit and blink their eyes,
Preferrin to philosophise.
Some Cats likes most folks pretty fine,
But some takes care to draw the line.
Some comes and rubs against you which,
Means will you scratch them where they itch,—
While others is so mean all through
They like lots better scratchin you.
And so you see the marvellous
Way Felines does resemble us,
Cats and Humans—all the same,
Jest sort of diff'rin in the name.

Anthony Henderson Euwer,
Christopher Cricket on Cats

SONNET TO MRS. REYNOLDS' CAT

Cat! who hast pass'd thy grand climacteric,
   How many mice and rats hast in thy days
   Destroy'd?—How many tit-bits stolen? Gaze
With those bright languid segments green, and prick
Those velvet ears—but pr'ythee do not stick
   Thy latent talons in me—and upraise
   Thy gentle mew—and tell me all thy frays
Of fish and mice, and rats and tender chick.
Nay, look not down, nor lick thy dainty wrists—
   For all the wheezy asthma,—and for all
Thy tail's tip is nick'd off—and though the fists
   Of many a maid have given thee many a maul,
Still is that fur as soft as when the lists
   In youth thou enter'dst on glass bottled wall.

John Keats

130

IN HONOR OF TAFFY TOPAZ

Taffy, the topaz-coloured cat,
Thinks now of this and now of that,
But chiefly on his meals.
Asparagus, and cream, and fish,
Are objects of his Freudian wish;
What you don't give, he steals.

His gallant heart is strongly stirred
By clink of plate or flight of bird,
He has a plumy tail;
At night he treads on stealthy pad
As merry as Sir Galahad
A-seeking of the Grail.

His amiable amber eyes
Are very friendly, very wise;
Like Buddha, grave and fat,
He sits, regardless of applause,
And thinking, as he kneads his paws,
What fun to be a cat!

Christopher Morley,
Songs for a Little House

132

SEVENTH CATERWAUL

How lucky to be a cat
Free to accept or—refuse
What is offered!

Walter Leon Hess,
Feline Philosophy

IF I HAD A CAT

A cat or a dog is something to play with, something to protect, something to bully, something to be dependent on you; something to sympathize with you, to abolish solitude, to take a lenient view of you, to have no secrets from, to talk to without being too well understood; something to observe, to study the primitive instincts in, to remind you of your high place in creation; even—not to shrink from sentiment—something to love.

H. W. Fowler,
If Wishes Were Horses

WHAT COULD IT BE?

I really do not like that cat;
I don't know why, it's maybe that
She's vicious, cruel, rude, ungrateful,
Smelly, treacherous, and hateful,
Supercilious, stupid, eerie,
Thoroughly boring, dull, and dreary,
Scheming, cold, and unproductive,
Inconvenient and destructive—
But most, I've just a *feeling* that
I *really* do not like that cat!

William Cole,
A Cat-Hater's Handbook

THE KITTEN

The trouble with a kitten is
THAT
Eventually it becomes a
CAT.

Ogden Nash,
Verses from 1929 On

CATS

. . . he neither toils nor spins, he is a parasite on you but he does not love you; he would die, cease to exist, vanish from the earth (I mean, in his so-called domestic form) but so far he has not had to. (There is the fable, Chinese I think, literary I am sure: of a period on earth when the dominant creatures were cats: who after ages of trying to cope with the anguishes of mortality—famine, plague, war, injustice, folly, greed—in a word, civilized government—convened a congress of the wisest cat philosophers to see if anything could be done: who after long delibera-tion agreed that the dilemma, the problems themselves were insoluble and the only practical solution was to give it up, relinquish, abdicate, by selecting from among the lesser creatures a species, race optimistic enough to believe that the mortal predicament could be solved and ig-norant enough never to learn better. Which is why the cat lives with you, is completely dependent on you for food and shelter but lifts no paw for you and loves you not; in a word, why your cat looks at you the way it does.)

William Faulkner,
The Reivers

THE CAT'S SERIOUSNESS

Among the things that kittens hate,
  A doll comes almost first:
'Tis bad enough to share its plate,
  To wear its clothes is worst.

Luxurious or dignified
  No kitten ever looked,
With bonnet strings severely tied,
  And cloak severely hooked.

E. V. Lucas,
A Cat Book

140

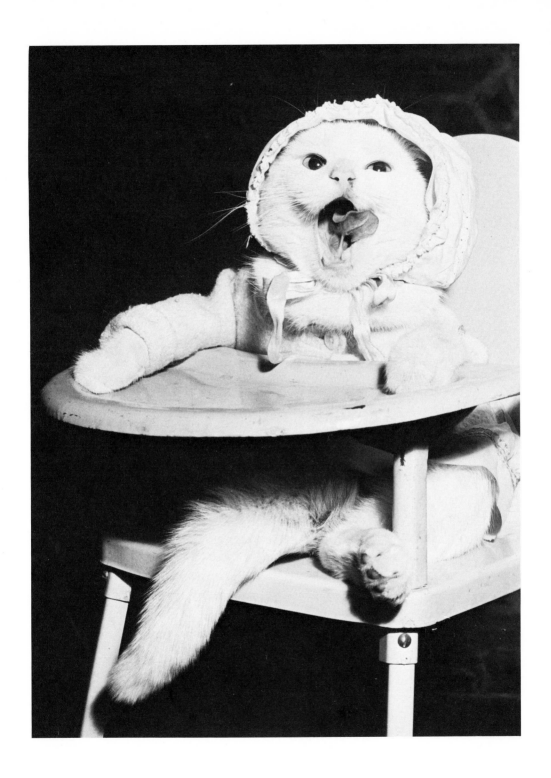

mehitabel meets her mate

tis the right of a modern tabby to choose
the cats who shall father her kits
and its nice to be sure their pasts have been pure
and theyre free from fleas or fits

trial marriage i tried till i thoroughly tired
and i suffered somewhat from abduction
and my heart it was broken again and again
but twas excellent instruction

i always have been rather awesomely blest
with the instincts of a mother
and my life and my fate have been down to date
one kitten after another

triplets quadruplets quintuplets
in a most confusing succession
and it seems to keep up whether times are good
or wallowing in depression

and this is in spite of the terrible fact
i am not a real home body
but an artiste who views the domestic career
as damnably dull and shoddy

for i am a lady who has her whims
no tom cat holds my love
if i come to feel i have plighted my troth
to a little mauve turtle dove

but at last i have found my real romance
through the process of trial and error
and he is a ribald brute named bill
one eyed and a holy terror

his skull is ditched from a hundred fights
and he has little hair on his tail
but the son of a gun of a brindled hun
is indubitably male. . . .

don marquis,
the lives and times
of archy and mehitabel

KRAZY: REFLECTION NO. 1

Two years ago if anyone
Had said I'd do what since I've done;
If anyone had told me that
I'd leave my chair to let a cat
Out of the house at seven-ten,
And rise to let her in again
At seven-twelve, and let her out
At seven-sixteen or thereabout,
And rise once more to weary feet
The whole performance to repeat
At seven-eighteen and -twenty-two
I should have answered, "Nerts to you!"
And "Nerts!" I should have sneered again.

But that was then. Ah, that was then!

Baron Ireland,
Our Cat

UNCANNY

There is something so peculiar in a cat's mysterious ways,
  That I'm inclined to think I hit the mark
In hinting at affinities with beings we can't praise,
  And do not like to think of after dark.

Have you noted, a cosy winter evening, in your chair,
  You would start up with a sudden, "Oh, dear me!"
As you caught, intently gazing at a thing that wasn't there,
  The feline member of your family?

Have you noticed how she listens with a sharp and anxious ear?
  And how she moves her head along the wall?
And you get so very nervous at the things you cannot hear,
  That you hardly dare to go to bed at all.

It is only that her senses, preternaturally keen,
  At night are very, very wide-awake;
And she looks at trifling shadows on the ceiling or the screen,
  That our dull, human vision does not take.

For the very softest footfall of a mouse in distant wall,
  Does not escape that most attentive ear,
Which is tuned to fine accordance far beyond our human call.
  Yet it sometimes makes us feel a little queer.

I wish they wouldn't do so, for it isn't very nice
  To have attention drawn from pleasant book,
And nervously imagine—when they only think of mice—
  And feel a strange sensation, when they *look*.

Elliot Walker,
Cat Tales in Verse

SINGULAR ATTACHMENTS

The cat, like many other animals, will often form singular attachments. One would sit in my horse's manger and purr and rub against his nose, which undoubtedly the horse enjoyed, for he would frequently turn his head purposely to be so treated. One went as consort with a Dorking cock; another took a great liking to my collie, Rover; another loved Lina, the cow; while another would cosset up close to a sitting hen, and allowed the fresh-hatched chickens to seek warmth by creeping under her. Again, they will rear other animals such as rats, rabbits, squirrels, puppies, hedgehogs; and, when motherly inclined, will take to almost anything, even to a young pigeon.

Harrison Weir,
Our Cats and All About Them

CORPORATION CATS

Cats are the only animals which are ever really owned by clubs and corporations. A dog, if it nominally belongs to a company of men, is really the property of some individual man. It must have a master. A cat, being always its own master, lives happily under a corporate body. Some of the lordliest and most self-satisfied beasts I have ever known were club and college cats. A cat belonging to one of the London dock companies was almost ridiculous (if a cat could be ridiculous) from the airs of possession and self-importance which it assumed in regard to the company's vaults. Sir Frederick Pollock has shown us, in the "Senior Fellow," to what a pitch of dignity a college cat may rise when it is once on the foundation of a learned society.

The Spectator

151

THE FRIENDSHIP OF A CAT

It is no easy task to win the friendship of a cat. He is a philosopher, sedate, tranquil, a creature of habit, a lover of decency and order. He does not bestow his regard lightly, and, though he may consent to be your companion, he will never be your slave. Even in his most affectionate moods he preserves his freedom, and refuses a servile obedience. But once gain his absolute confidence, and he is a friend for life. He shares your hours of work, of solitude, of·melancholy. He spends whole evenings on your knee, purring and dozing, content with your silence, and spurning for your sake the society of his kind. In vain loud miaulings from the neighbouring roof summon him to those choice entertainments where red herrings take the place of tea. He pays no heed, and cannot be tempted from your side. If you put him down, he leaps back again, mewing a gentle protest. From time to time he looks into your face with eyes so human, so full of understanding and regard, that you are smitten by fear. Can it be possible that there is not thought behind that absorbed and mysterious scrutiny?

Théophile Gautier,
Menagerie Intime

PRACTICE

Cultivate your garden, said Goethe and Voltaire,
Every other task is wasted and dead-born;
Narrow all your efforts to a given sphere,
Seek your Heaven daily in a bit of ground.

So my cat behaves. Like a veteran,
He brushes well his coat before he sits to dine;
All his work is centred in his own domain,
Just to keep his spotless fur soft, and clean, and fine.

His tongue is sponge, and brush, and towel, and curry-
  comb,
Well he knows what work it can be made to do,
Poor little wash-rag, smaller than my thumb.

His nose touches his back, touches his hind paws too,
Every patch of fur is raked, and scraped, and smoothed;
What more has Goethe done, what more could Voltaire do?

Hippolyte Taine

A HOME WITHOUT A CAT

A home without a cat—and a well-fed, well-petted and properly revered cat—may be a perfect home, perhaps, but how can it prove its title?

Mark Twain

MY CAT

Deep in my brain walks to and fro,
As well as in his own domain,
A handsome cat of gentle strain,—
Scarce can I hear his mew so low.

His tender call wakes not alarm,
But though he growl or softly sound,
Still is his voice rich and profound,—
There lies his secret and his charm.

No other bow can ever bring
From my heart's perfect instrument
Such royal notes of deep content
Or waken its most vibrant string.

Than can thy voice, mysterious Puss,
Seraphic cat, and cat most strange,
As a celestial, scorning change,
As subtle as harmonious.

With growing wonderment I see
The fire in thy pale pupils glow
Like watch lights when the sun is low,
Thy living opals gaze at me.

Charles Pierre Baudelaire

AMUSE A CAT

Everything that moves, serves to interest and amuse a cat. He is convinced that nature is busying herself with his diversion; he can conceive of no other purpose in the universe; and when we sport with him, and make him leap and tumble, he probably takes us for pantomimists and buffoons.

F. A. Paradis de Moncrif

THE CAT OF EGYPT

The number of domestic animals in Egypt is very great, and would be still greater, were it not for what befalls the cats. As the females, when they have kittened, no longer seek the company of the males, these last, to obtain once more their companionship, practise a curious artifice. They seize the kittens, carry them off, and kill them; but do not eat them afterwards. Upon this, the females, being deprived of their young, and longing to supply their place, seek the males once more, since they are particularly fond of their offspring.

On every occasion of a fire in Egypt, the strangest prodigy occurs with the cats. The inhabitants allow the fire to rage as it pleases, while they stand about at intervals and watch these animals, which, slipping by the men, or else leaping over them, rush headlong into the flames. When this happens, the Egyptians are in deep affliction. If a cat dies in a private house by a natural death, all the inmates of the house shave their eyebrows. The dead cats are taken to the city of Bubastis, where they are embalmed, after which they are buried in certain sacred repositories.

Herodotus

A cat is nobody's fool. . . .

Heywood Broun,
It Seems to Me

161

CATS ARE LIKE WOMEN

Cats are like women, and women are like
cats. They are both very ungrateful.

Damon Runyon,
Guys and Dolls

THE EARLY BIRD

They say the Early Bird the Worm shall taste.
Then rise, O Kitten! Wherefore, sleeping, waste
The fruits of Virtue? Quick! the Early Bird
Will soon be on the flutter—O make haste!

The Early Bird has gone, and with him ta'en
The Early Worm—Alas! the Moral's plain,
O Senseless Worm! Thus, thus we are repaid
for Early Rising—I shall doze again.

Oliver Herford,
The Rubaiyat of a Persian Kitten

FARM CATS

The life of cats about a farm is in itself worthy of a whole study. They come and go from one set of farm buildings to another, according, so far as I am able to make out, to the rise and fall of food supplies. No animal but a hog knows better how to take care of himself. We have a score of farm cats, fat and sleek and well fed on mice, rats and unwary sparrows, as well as on the milk from the dairy barn and the table scraps from the houses. In summer some of the big toms will take to the fields and thickets leading a sporting life and living off the countryside. More than once when mowing, I have started up out of the thick hay a big tom engaged in stalking field mice. I don't like it when they take young birds and chipmunks but there doesn't seem to be any way of controlling them and in the barns they are not only valuable but indispensable, prowling the rooms, the feed mows and the cattle stalls to keep down vermin. The number which "goes wild" in summer is small for they are well fed in the barns and find an easy living there and at the kitchen doors of the various houses.

As a rule the barn cats are just cats and it is sometimes difficult to distinguish one from another, but occasionally there develops what might be described in Rotarian language as an "outstanding" cat. You begin to notice something different about such a cat, and discern certain quirks of personality or behavior which attract your notice and you begin to have a special feeling for him and watch him and give a closer observation to his behavior.

Louis Bromfield,
Animals and Other People

THE MOST PERFECT OF CARNIVORES

The degree of perfection reached by any living organism is simply the amount of specialization or adaptation which it has undergone in its relations to the special natural conditions under which its life is passed, and measured by this standard, the cat is the most perfect of carnivores. Feeding upon other animals, which it must pursue with noiseless stealth and capture by an exertion of supreme activity, the cat has padded feet which make no sound in movement; muscles of enormous power and bulk in proportion to its size, and attached to bones addressed to each other at such angles as to form the most complete system of springs and levers for propelling the body known in the whole group; the claws are sharper and curved into strong hooks more than in any other mammal, and by the action of special muscles are withdrawn under the protection of sheathlike pads, that they may escape wear and injury when not in use; no teeth are better fitted for their work—the great canines for tearing, and the scissor-like premolars for shearing off lumps of flesh small enough to swallow; while the short and simple alimentary tract takes up little internal space, and permits of a lithe and slender form suited to the highest activity, at the same time performing its digestive work rapidly, and soon ridding the animal of the burden of the enormous meals which those which feed only when they can are certain to indulge in when the opportunity arises.

Rush Shippen Huidekoper, M.D.,
The Cat

A LEAVETAKING

Today I said good-bye to Cinnamon, my ginger tabby cat, who had shared his life with me for almost thirteen years. The pain is everywhere. It was an unexpected farewell. A sudden lameness had slowed his gait, always dignified and measured, but no one anticipated the diagnosis: osteosarcoma, metastasized to the lungs. Prognosis negative. I knew the decision I had to make—as many had made before me—but the kind veterinarian didn't hurry me. "I'll be glad to send the X rays to the University of California at Davis for corroboration, but I'm pretty positive that's what it is. There is already a traumatic fracture in that left leg." He left me alone in the examining room, and I wept as though I were losing my best friend. And I was.

I had had Cinnamon's mother and uncle first—for a time all three—then Cinnamon and a matching red Persian, Jason—and for the last year and a half Cinnamon and I had shared our home with Beckett, the Himalayan. We had shared so much else, too. Friends who came (and sometimes went), but who stopped to pat with real affection the huge, shy orange cat whose only expression, according to one friend, was adoring. And all during the last years of my mother's life he had climbed into her lap, hanging over the edges, but perfectly content. Or had stood by her chair in the dining room, waiting for a tidbit that was always offered at the end of the meal. Cinnamon never begged. He was a most polite cat. Every morning he sat on the kitchen floor beside my chair as I finished breakfast, waiting for the cereal dish to be lowered to the floor for him to lap up the last few drops of cream. I never took a nap that he didn't jump up to the bed to lie down beside me, his weight hard against my leg or back, purring his quiet restrained purr, befitting an elderly gentleman whose manners were impeccable.

He was a timid cat with strangers. A party sent him scooting under the bed, where he sometimes stayed until the last unfamiliar voice was gone. He was particularly wary of deep male voices. Women made friends with him more easily. He climbed into their laps, kneading the place to make it more his, then settling his fifteen pounds on their well-pressed skirts and closing his eyes to slits. To remove him seemed profoundly ungracious, though he never made a fuss.

In the last few years of his life he slept a great deal, either in his basket or on my bed or in the newly upholstered chair he had claimed

169

for his own. Only when Beckett, in his kittenish enthusiasm, hopped on him from chair or couch, urging him to play tag, did he loosen up his old joints for a romp. Then the two of them tore through the house, threatening the lamps, the Oriental art objects, the candlesticks. Once, only a few months ago, I saw him race up the avocado tree, Beckett in the lead. Often such exertions brought on a fit of coughing.

But nothing marred his appetite. He was on hand night and morning for his bowl of food. He ate with his left paw, daintily lifting the food out and putting it in his mouth. If he didn't like the selection that day, he often dropped a piece into his water as silent protest. For milk he had a special miaow, and a warm bowlful was his favorite chaser to breakfast.

With children he was especially gentle, allowing the small ones to lug him around like a sack. He was so big they could hardly lift him, but if they sat on the floor he could crawl into their laps. He never scratched a person—only the dining room Oriental rug, which was his in a definitive way no one could argue with. For the scratching post he had a fine disdain.

At night he slept in the study in his wicker basket, only climbing down when I opened the door to say good morning. His small voice, totally out of character with his bulk, replied politely, and we were ready to begin the day.

Tomorrow he won't be here to help me. When I said good-bye to him today in the doctor's office, I tried to tell him what he had meant to me for all those years, but of course I couldn't. One can never express the full measure of love. I could only scratch him between the ears where he loved it best and kiss him there and tell him what a very special cat he had always been—the most loving, the most loyal, the most patient with my impatience, the most trusting and devoted. "You were not just a good cat," I told him, "you were a great cat, Cinnamon. And we had happy years together. Now you have fulfilled your cat-ness. And this is the last thing I can do for you, to spare you suffering and a miserable death. That much I can do, though it breaks my heart." He looked up at my face and miaowed questioningly. I caressed his head and ears again and turned away. I couldn't see him for the tears.

In every loss are all past losses. I weep for Cinnamon, my cat, and the deaths that have gone before.

Jean Burden

THE THINKING CAT

A cat appears to do nothing and is yet
an able servant; though he speak but
little, yet he thinks the more.

Baron Ludwig Holberg

THE CAT

I like the simple dignity
  That hedges round the cat;
You never see her showing off,
  She lets the dog do that.

You never catch her leaping hoops,
  Nor prancing on the floor
Upon two legs, when generous
  Dame Nature gave her four.

We train the dog to hunt the birds,
  And beat him when he fails.
He works all day, and never gets
  A single taste of quails.

The cat is wiser far than he,
  She hunts for birds to eat;
She does not run her legs off, just
  To give some man a treat.

All cats, no matter what their breed,
  Are born aristocrats;
They never, like the terriers, make
  A trade of killing rats.

The cat will rid the house of rats,
  Because she likes the fun,
No man can say she's moved to it,
  Because he wants it done.

Man harnesses the lightning, and
  Makes steam perform his will,
The horse and dog his bond-slaves are,
  The cat eludes him still.

The dog's man's servant, plaything, drudge,
   A foolish altruist;
The cat, in spite of man, remains
   Serene, an egotist.

Talk not to me about your dog,
   It is but idle chat;
Give me that calm philosopher
   Of hearth and home, the cat.

Ruth Kimball Gardiner

DISCIPLINE

A female cat is kept young in spirit and supple in body by the restless vivacity of her kittens. She plays with her little ones, fondles them, pursues them if they roam too far, and corrects them sharply for all the faults to which feline infancy is heir. A kitten dislikes being washed quite as much as a child does, especially in the neighbourhood of its ears. It tries to escape the infliction, rolls away, paddles with its little paws, and behaves as naughtily as it knows how, until a smart slap brings it suddenly back to subjection. Pussy has no confidence in moral suasion, but implicitly follows Solomon's somewhat neglected advice. I was once told a pleasant story of an English cat who had reared several large families, and who, dozing one day before the nursery fire, was disturbed and annoyed by the whining of a fretful child. She bore it as long as she could, waiting for the nurse to interpose her authority; then, finding passive endurance had outstripped the limits of her patience, she arose, crossed the room, jumped on the sofa, and twice with her strong soft paw, which had chastised many an erring kitten, deliberately boxed the little girl's ears,—after which she returned to her slumbers.

Agnes Repplier,
The Fireside Sphinx

THE MOUSE'S HOLE

The cat, with eyne of burning coal,
Now couches fore the mouse's hole.

William Shakespeare,
Pericles

THE CONTEMPLATIVE LIFE

From the dawn of creation the cat has known his place, and he has kept it, practically untamed and unspoiled by man. He has *retenue*. Of all animals, he alone attains to the Contemplative Life. He regards the wheel of existence from without, like the Buddha. There is no pretence of sympathy about the cat. He lives alone, aloft, sublime, in a wise passiveness. He is excessively proud; and, when he is made the subject of conversation, will cast one glance of scorn, and leave the room in which personalities are bandied. All expressions of emotion he scouts as frivolous and insincere, except, indeed, in the ambrosial night, when, free from the society of mankind, he pours forth his soul in strains of unpremeditated art. The paltry pay and paltry praise of humanity he despises, like Edgar Poe. He does not exhibit the pageant of his bleeding heart; he does not howl when people die, nor explode in cries of delight when his master returns from a journey. With quiet courtesy, he remains in his proper and comfortable place, only venturing into view when something he approves of, such as fish or game, makes its appearance. On the rights of property he is firm. If a strange cat enters his domain, he is up in claws to resist invasion. It was for these qualities, probably, that the cat was worshipped by the ancient Egyptians.

Andrew Lang

177

PLAY IN ANIMALS

Play in animals is the preparation
for the business of their life.

Elbert Hubbard,
Pig-pen Pete

CAT LANGUAGE

The cat has the advantage of a language which has the same vowels as pronounced by the dog and with six consonants in addition: m, n, g, h, v and f. Consequently the cat has a greater number of words.

Dupont de Nemours

THE CAT'S CLAWS

Most interesting to the naturalist are the cat's claws. They are used to seize and hold the prey till the animal can get the better of it by biting it in the neck. They facilitate motion on steep inclines or slippery surfaces. They must therefore be flexible and capable of powerful grip. At the same time it must be possible to keep them out of the way when the foot is used for walking, and to prevent them from being blunted by continued contact with the ground. The muscular arrangement for protruding and retracting the claws provides for all these circumstances.

The fore-limbs have a freedom of motion about equal to that of the apes and monkeys. They can be stretched out, turned, can strike a blow as easily as can a man's fist. The tiger can smash the shoulder blade of an ox or buffalo at a single stroke and the domestic cat is, in her own realm, similarly efficient.

Georgina Stickland Gates,
The Modern Cat: Her Mind and Manners

CAT ON A STOVE

We should be careful to get out of an experience only the wisdom that is in it—and stop there: lest we be like the cat that sits on a hot stove-lid. She will never sit down on a hot stove-lid again—and that is well; but also she will never sit down on a cold one any more.

Mark Twain,
Following the Equator

185

CATS MAY HAVE NINE LIVES
BUT I HAVE ONLY ONE

Cats *like* me, be they known or strange,
Especially the ones with mange.
They love to leap into my lap
And settle for a nice long nap,
And when at last they leave my chair
They're generous indeed with hair.

Cats *like* me, those at least with paws
Equipped with extra-pointed claws.
They never miss a single chance
To frolic with my Sunday pants,
And do their best to make my serge
Look just like tweeds, or on the verge.

Cats *like* me, that is very clear,
And probably they think it's queer
That when they've shown themselves so fond,
I don't respond.

Richard Armour,
Nights with Armour

COURTING CATS

Cats are clean. Their personal cleanliness is directly related with their hunger. The better fed the cat, the cleaner he is. This is logical, since cats habitually wash after they have eaten. The more often a cat eats, the more often he will wash. If the cat has not eaten, as is the case with numerous homeless strays, it has no reason to wash.

About the only other time a cat that is normally clean will neglect his grooming is when he is sick or when he is courting. Actually, it is not the business of courtship that prevents the cat from washing, but his complete indifference to food during this period. Not having eaten, the cat won't wash.

It is probably during their courtship that cats do most to antagonize non-cat owners and some cat owners too. There is nothing more cacophonous and persistent than the lovemaking sounds of cats. If just the meows and howls of the male and female were heard, it wouldn't be too bad. Rarely, however, is just one male involved. One female, yes, but she will attract every male cat in the neighborhood.

We live in a rural area—in a one-mile radius there are about six other farms. We see no cats but ours all year long. But in mid-winter our females feel the call of the wild, and so do half a dozen males who come to court them. We have no idea where they live or how they know. But they know. And they let *us* know.

After mating, the females revert to their aloof, man-hating selves and will have nothing further to do with the Toms. The males will linger about hopefully for a week or so, but after being clawed by their erstwhile lovers, they take the hint and depart to conquer other hearts.

Walter Chandoha,
Walter Chandoha's Book of Kittens and Cats

TEACHING CATS TRICKS

Our family cat could understand forty different words and phrases. She could sit up, roll over, speak, come, go, fetch—and she kept learning things all her life. When she was sixteen she learned how to catch little pieces of cake in midair. One day we figured out how she was able to explore a totally unfamiliar area and always find her way back: she moved in gradually expanding concentric circles—first a very small circle that encompassed only our immediate locale, then another that took in a little more, until she enlarged the known territory to include everything she wished to investigate within practical hiking distance.

We thought her a remarkable cat, and I still think she was—but not as unusual as we thought then. We have since taken in many cats, often adults that have never known a home before, and, as a matter of interest, experimented to see how long it takes a cat, any cat, to learn to shake hands and sit up. The average, we found, to learn and remember it forever—or as far into forever as we have been able to follow—is nine minutes. This ability to learn quickly and respond to human commands is not widely recognized in cats, and one sometimes wonders if they have masked this from an instinctive knowledge that, as Franklin Roosevelt said, to some much is given, of others much is expected—and they would rather have their rendezvous with destiny in another format than a string of tricks endlessly and boringly repeated.

Yet it is not the tricks that are significant; it is the basis they set up for communication. Once a cat has learned that you are speaking to it directly and expect a certain result—"Shake!" "Sit up!"—it is possible to go on to even more meaningful and useful aspects of a cat-human dialogue, such as "No," "Here," "Wait," and so on.

Laura Riley

191

INDEX OF AUTHORS

INDEX OF TITLES